A Taste for Work
Your Menu to Career Success

Copyright © 2009 by Teri Clancy, Joy Maguire-Dooley, Sally Morrison

ISBN 978-0-557-08554-5

A Taste for Work
Your Menu to Career Success

Teri Clancy, Joy Maguire-Dooley,
Sally Morrison

Acknowledgements

We want to thank Jack Harms and for editing and proofreading to make our book sound and look professional.

Thank you to Rich Sanders for his technical expertise and generosity in setting up our website and answering endless computer questions.

Thanks to Falise Platt for her innovative ideas and continual support.

And of course, to our families and friends, we say thank you for your love and encouragement as we worked through our project. Over the years many have asked, "When are you going to write a book?" Without your gentle nudges, we may never have got all of our information together to put it into a book.

Finally, none of this would have been possible without our job seekers. Thank you for finding our services and trusting our advice. We dedicate this book to all of you!

Contents

Acknowledgements v

Introduction ix

Chapter 1
Healing and Comfort…Nurture Yourself 1

Chapter 2
Assessments…The Appetizer 13

Chapter 3
Resumes…Soup – not – Salad 33

Chapter 4
Networking…Don't Be Chicken 67

Chapter 5
Interviews…The Main Course 95

Chapter 6
How to Find the Jobs…Side Dishes 131

Chapter 7
Getting the Offer and the Money…Ready for Dessert? ... 151

Chapter 8
The First 90 Days…Trying Something New 163

Now Get Going 173

Introduction

This book brings you 50 years of combined experience in the career development field. We have even more years of experience in the kitchen. Combine all those years and you can develop *A Taste for Work* just by reading along.

We are three women who have raised families, helped people find jobs, started new careers, opened new businesses, been promoted, learned to navigate work politics and knew when it was time to move on.

We have heard and seen just about everything while trekking through life with hard work, education, nurturing spirits and good food. We know what works and what doesn't when it comes to jobs, careers, life's work, and comfort. We've learned a lot.

By reading this book, you can benefit from our experience and learn about self-reliant career development through self-awareness, self-help, and self-care. We offer tried and true practical information to guide you to your next job or point you toward career advancement. If you are not happy with the work you are doing now or if you are looking for a new job, this book is for you.

Just as food is essential for our lives, job search skills are basic to career self-reliance. We offer the fundamentals—a process that works.

We have included recipes in our career book because food is the most practical form of self-care. It sustains you, gives you energy, and keeps you going. We chose dishes that will nourish your body and soothe your soul. You will find a variety of recipes including healthy choices, delicious old-fashioned comfort food, and quick meal ideas.

So then, this is a book that combines the best practices for career self-reliance; directions for navigating through the maze of career directions and job search tools and tips for cooking up some good food along the way. We want you to become more aware of how you operate, how you can help yourself and how to give good self-care.

In addition to being career mentors, we are mothers. We have raised kids and watched their successes. We have cheered for them in their triumphs and propped them up in their disappointments. We have done it with sugar cookies, chicken noodle soup, or hot chocolate. We know what sustains people over long and sometimes turbulent journeys. Good food sure helps.

We want this book to serve as a resource for making choices about yourself and your future. You can go fast and speed read, or you can read awhile, put our book down, and pick it up a few days later. It is about your choices and about being okay to go at your own pace. We believe you to be creative, resourceful, and capable of making good decisions for yourself. Feel free to do just that. Give yourself permission to experience this book in any way you believe will best serve you, your career direction, and your life.

Give yourself freedom to dream and create a plan to be all you can be. What a perfect time to take the path less traveled and see what you might have missed along the way. Enjoy the experience!

Because you've picked up this book, it's likely you have a concern about your career. You may be looking for a job, thinking about looking for a job or just feeling generally uncomfortable in your current work. You are not alone. Studies show 98% of Americans are not happy with their jobs. Most of us experience some level of discontent at work. If you fit into that category, you have a lot of company.

But watch it! This book isn't just about finding a new job. It's about career development, and career development is about more than replacing a lost job. Having a career and having a job are not the same. Did you know that according to the Department of Labor, recent college graduates can expect to hold eleven to thirteen jobs in three to five different career fields and remain in each job for just two and half years? Creating a successful work life now requires planning and strategy. There is no more joining Dad at the firm. More than likely, there is a buy out at the firm, Dad is downsized, and he is struggling, too.

Let's face it; change is a constant in every aspect of life. Corporations are smaller, leaner, and meaner. Global competition is razor sharp. Middle management as it once was has all but disappeared. People even dress differently at work. You will be changing jobs, changing career direction and getting promoted in this "new" culture. Now is the time to begin to develop a strategy that will sustain you for the rest of your work life.

You must plan and strategize about what work you want to do; plan and strategize your job search; plan and strategize ways to make the best of every opportunity; plan and strategize for moving to each successive opportunity. Central to your success is being able to capitalize on every single skill and asset you have and continually be looking for skills and assets to develop.

We're here to show you how. This is not a book about re-inventing yourself. This is a book about *defining* yourself. You don't have to become a different person to develop the career you want. You are good to go just as you are. However, we may ask you to change your thinking a little. We want you to be the person you are and use the information we offer in the best ways you can.

We will give you great ideas for ways to use your talent and assets, and we will show you how to eat well while you are doing it. Then we will send you out there to make it work, taking along all you have learned in this book. We call it "kicking you in the assets while filling your stomach."

We ask you to read this book actively, with the goal of using its practical suggestions to develop and fuel yourself as well as your career. Use our blueprint for career development and our guidelines for the mechanics of job search. Try the recipes to support you in exhaustion, in disappointment and in success. Know that, from cover to cover, it is our intention to support and nurture you through your ups and downs and we have slipped in some motherly tough love along the way.

Chapter 1

Healing and Comfort...Nurture Yourself

Your first inclination may be to skip this chapter when you see it is all about dealing with loss. But while it may not be a fun exercise, it is crucial to a successful career development plan. Really, this chapter is also about finding some comfort and solace as well. In fact, at the end of it, you will find some of our favorite comfort recipes. They are dishes we like to whip up when we are feeling a little needy and require some soothing and consoling. We think they will work for you, too.

It would be great if we could follow with a recipe to work through the grief process of losing a job. Unfortunately, this is one of those times when your Mom's method of cooking by adding "a little bit of this" and "and a little bit of that" works better.

Each of us comes to job loss from a slightly different experience base. Although our grief and loss differ in the same way the temperature of ovens vary, it is still painful and hard to endure. Some of us are angry about the way we left our last job. Some of us are relieved--even glad. There are as many feelings as there are people. Each feeling is correct. Take ownership of that feeling. No one has the right to tell you how to feel. How we act and react, however, does have an impact on others and our own future career development.

Consider setting aside some time in the beginning of your transition (or right now if you haven't already done this) for grieving. Give yourself the gift of time. Perhaps a long weekend, a week, whatever works for you. Think of it as a healing, gentle time, a period when you nurture yourself physically and emotionally. What? You don't have the time to do this. You don't have the time *not* to do this! Dealing with a job loss is one of the basic building blocks of career development and we want to give you some ideas of how to do it.

The pain from a loss can be physical. Counter this pain with a physical activity.

- Go for a walk in the woods, by a lake or the ocean. Feel the calm or the ebb and flow of nature.
- Plant a garden. Dig in the dirt. Digging and feeling the earth is probably one of the best exercises for loss there is.
- Read a book. Lose yourself in it.
- Play or listen to music-something soothing or upbeat. Paint, create sculpture, finger paint. Make sand castles.
- Rent a funny movie. Laugh!
- Hang out with your children or grandchildren or friends and play. Blow bubbles. It is hard to frown when you're blowing bubbles. Shoot water guns, jump rope, try whistling down the lane, do Legos or puzzles.

There are executives who never gave in to the grieving process. Lay off is on a Friday. Monday morning they are back on the 6:20 AM train into the city. They had their briefcases in their hands pretending nothing had changed.

What would the neighbors say if they knew these executives had lost their jobs? What would their families say? Their train buddies? After a few weeks of this charade, the executives found out what their neighbors would say. When the neighbors learned the truth, these people became their best allies. Their employed friends were more than willing to share information. They wanted to help. They just needed to be asked.

But even more important than getting the help is taking some time to "get off the train," unwind and prepare for the next steps. You aren't afraid are you? Great! Then let's get to it and through it and on with the job search.

But set the record straight right up front. Grieving is indeed a process, but not a linear one. You might feel great and energized one day and then down in the dumps the next. This is normal and you should plan for it. When you are on a high, this is the time to move ahead and take some action. When those down times hit, step back and do something that nurtures you. This process is similar to following a road without a map. You move forward, you stop, you move backward, you stop and then you move forward again--and yes, you might stop again along the way. We cannot say it enough: This is a natural part of the grieving process and life as a whole. There will always be an ebb and flow. You have to wait for the flow and know this ebb will pass.

The loss process often duplicates itself. You lose something; you grieve and eventually move on. Then, you have another loss and the entire grieving process starts all over again. Sometimes the emotions are more intense than they were with your original loss.

Each of us carries an "emotional well" that we use to store our losses. Every loss holds a certain amount of grief for you. The amount varies for each person and for each event.

When a loss occurs, depending on its severity and importance to you, some of your grief is poured into your well. You lose your car keys, you pour in a thimble full. Your dog dies, you pour in a bucket full. You lose your job, you get divorced, you have a serious illness, a family member dies, and there may be several buckets that need dumping into your well.

At some point, your well fills up because loss is cumulative. As you can imagine, this topping off point occurs at different times for different people. That is one of the reasons a job loss affects individuals differently. For some, it occurs when their well is full and the dumping causes a spillover. For others, there's still room in their well.

Once the well of losses spills over, you may start grieving former losses or events you thought you had laid to rest. A man called the other day wondering if he was "going over the edge." His mother had died six months ago, and while he had cried and grieved, he was quickly back at work. A week before calling us, he had lost his job and had been unable to stop crying for the entire seven days. "I certainly didn't care more about my job than my Mom. Why am I so upset about losing the job and less so about losing my mother? I do feel guilty about not crying more for my Mom, and I'm ashamed. But I just want to stop crying."

When we explained the well theory, he felt better. His well had filled to the top, and when it spilled over with his job loss, he began grieving the past loss of his mother even more.

You need to know where you are in the grieving process. It's a relief to know so much of what you're experiencing is natural and will occur without your awareness or knowledge. But we are resilient beyond our expectation. We can withstand torture and destruction when necessary. Paradoxically, we are also fragile and can feel great hurt. It's necessary that you be aware of both halves of your person and nurture each equally.

Psychiatrist and world-renowned author Elisabeth Kubler-Ross introduced the five stages of grief. While initially these feelings apply to people facing death, the five stages of grieving are now applied to any loss large or small. Here we are talking about life changing loss. These stages are not to be static, but ebb and flow process with, hopefully, an eventual resolution.

The five stages are:

- Denial: "This can't be happening to me."
- Anger: "Why is this happening to me? Who is to blame?"
- Bargaining: "Make this not happen and in return I will _____."
- Depression: "I'm too sad to do anything."
- Acceptance: (This is where we deviate from the pro.) We prefer the word author Darcy Simms uses: Acknowledgement or "to admit as true" versus "to agree to." You may or may not like that this has happened, but you admit that it has and you are ready to move on.

Don't expect these stages to go in order. Some people even skip a stage. Some go back and forth among stages. Some move through all five like clockwork. There is no right or wrong in this process. There is no timetable for grief. While some people take weeks to move on, others take months. Be aware where you are. That is the key. Don't judge yourself by others.

Each process is unique. Wouldn't it be great if we could stick ourselves with a toothpick to see when we were done? Not going to happen, so just be aware of your feelings. They will let you know. Only be concerned if you are stuck in one stage and are unable to move on. A good indicator would be if you were immobilized or completely overwhelmed and not sure which way to turn. If that happens, seek professional help. Look for a mental health professional with some background in loss and grief.

Allow yourself to experience this process. If you have lost your job, you might miss the daily routine of getting up and getting off to work. That routine is gone now. The co-workers are gone as well. You might miss the culture of work. There are no meetings to attend, no interesting conversations regarding how you are going to close the next sale.

Job loss also hits your social life. Suddenly there are no co-workers to talk with about sports or movies. There is no one to invite to try out the new lunch entrée at the local restaurant. There are only people who ask you what you do for a living and you have no answer.

Maybe you were downsized, your whole department was cut, and you had nothing to say about it. One day you are here, the next day you are gone. Are you angry? Depressed? Anxious?

The more emotionally invested you were in your job the deeper the mourning will be. Often a job carries a lot of personal identity and many people feel they have lost a piece of themselves when a job is lost or a career seems exhausted. Mourning the loss of this part of you through the grieving process is now part of your new work. No one can do this for you. This is up to *you*. This might be the hardest job you have ever done. But if you picked up this book, chances are you are up to this challenge.

As we go through the stages in a little more depth, think about your life. Become aware of where you are right now.

The first phase of grief is denial. "This can't be happening to me." "Other people get downsized and let go." "I did such a good job." "They would never let me go." "They made a mistake." "They'll call me back." There is denial that this loss really occurred. It isn't happening. If I keep getting up in the morning and going out, I will be working I have not really lost my job. De Nile ain't just a river in Egypt.

Phase Two of the grieving process is anger. This stage can cause the most pain for you and others. You might say hurtful things to yourself and those close to you. Attempting to repress or stifle this emotion does not make it go away. What we resist persists. It often surfaces inappropriately late. Deal with the emotion before it comes back in a stronger and fiercer way.

Phase Three of the grieving process is bargaining. At this stage, anger has passed and desperation has set in. We look for ways to avoid or change what has happened. Bargaining is an unproductive demonstration of hope that the employer will change his mind. If you really feel desperate, you might offer to take a cut in salary, give up some benefits, or accept a demotion. These actions generally do not work and end up leaving you feeling depressed. It is unlikely you would even have the chance to bargain the loss. It may have happened so quickly bargaining was an option only in your imagination.

Phase Four of the grieving process is depression. This can be the most dangerous stage. Everyone goes through some depression before he can deal with a major loss. It is real and a natural part of life. Remember, the deeper the attachment the longer the depression can be. There is always light at the end of a long dark tunnel. Look for that light.

And Finally, the last phase is acceptance or acknowledgement. Don't expect any bells or whistles here. This is when you realize that no amount of denial, anger, bargaining, or depression is going to bring the job back. You must make peace with the way things are. It's now time to move on.

To help you work through this process, we have come up with a formula of helpful hints. We like to think of it as a recipe for successfully mourning your loss.

- Since the grieving process can be isolating and depressing, get outside your house! Get out in the land of the living when you are feeling defeated or stressed. Join with others in a support group or accountability group. Go to a networking event or career center. You will soon see this is not about you. This is about an event. Look around you. This has happened to others. You are not alone.

- Design a new daily routine. A routine can bring clarity and focus. Have a daily calendar with at least three job action items on it. For example, send four resumes, make four networking calls. Include your life action items, like picking the kids up from soccer or going to the grocery store.

- Set some time each day to feel negative. Assign a time to do that. Crazy as it sounds, it will keep your negativity to a minimum. For example: a negative thought about your former boss creeps into your head. Say to yourself, "Self, I'll address my boss and all the other negatives in my life at 4 PM." You are not repressing it, just deferring it. At 4 PM, sit down and write all the negatives that came at you during the day. At 4:30, get up and make Kindergarten Cookies (see recipe at the end of this chapter) or take the dog for a walk. The next day do the same thing. Pretty soon, your negative thoughts will no longer rule you and you'll have some great cookies to take to a networking event. Meanwhile, you have soothed yourself and acknowledged your feelings. as well

- As part of your routine, keep a journal of your feelings and write down the positive and negative. Studies show those who journal get through the job search process, including grieving the loss of the job, 15 percent more quickly than those who did not. End each journal exercise by writing down a few things for which you are grateful. You will start to see you have more reasons for gratitude than you realized. This is also a good exercise before you go to bed each night. Thinking of positive things instead of listening to the news (which is usually negative) can only work in your favor.

- Surround yourself with positive people. You will encounter people who want to help. Perhaps some do not know how, but they give you positive feedback and energy. Lose those who cause you to feel negative
- Try helping others. Volunteer somewhere or just be present for another person in need. You might have lost your job, but not your ability to give of yourself for the good of others. More about this later.
- Look for positives around you. Avoid listening to the media for long durations. The media tends to focus on the negative. Keep your social life active. Do things you enjoy. Be creative and find low cost or free things to energize you.
- Last, but certainly not least, evaluate your diet and exercise plan. Vigorous exercise done regularly can help eliminate stress. It also helps you relax and stay focused. Doing it with a friend, it increases your sense of belonging. A healthy diet also promotes a general sense of well-being.

Comfort and reward are important components in career transition. Food often plays a part.

- We can get energized with food
- We can get creative preparing food for ourselves, family and friends
- We can share recipes with others creating networking opportunities
- We can make healthy choices around food
- We can help others feel comforted by bringing them food

Grief can help you change course in your life. Sometimes we have to be knocked off our horse to get the message to change directions. Sometimes we just don't see it. If there is a message at all in this story, it is to be open to what the universe tells you. You don't always know what to do with that message, but eventually you will find out. Help is available to work through the logistics of what comes next. You alone are the one to recognize and decipher the message when it comes, and it surely will.

A case in point:

Joy was in Public Relations doing a decent job but not thrilled with the work when her parents became ill with cancer. Both of them. Joy and her sister took turns going to New Jersey to care for their parents over a three-month period. Through this experience, Joy learned what it meant to die with dignity. Her parents were great teachers right up until their deaths…17 days apart.

Joy's parents lived on the beach in New Jersey with a magnificent ocean at their doorstep. No trees, just miles and miles of sandy beach.

On one of Joy's weekly trips to New Jersey, the flight was horrific. People were screaming as they were tossed about in the air. Joy was trying to eat lunch and read a book called, *The Fall of Freddie the Leaf* but it was impossible to do either during the bumpy flight. The man sitting beside Joy was very calm so she asked him if he was a pilot and if he knew something about the conditions that were not evident to her. His response stunned her: "God isn't done with you yet, and since I am sitting beside you I'm okay."

When the flight landed, people cheered and hugged one another. Joy shook the man's hand and said, "I guess I am getting ready to do something, eh?" He said, "You are and good luck." Joy was confused. What was that supposed to mean? By the way, before going on to her parents, Joy stopped and had a comforting bowl of chicken noodle soup.

That night she read the book *The Fall of Freddie the Leaf* to her father. It is a story about a leaf that is afraid to let go of the tree. Eventually Freddie dies and drops to the ground and then he gets to see the whole picture--that he is part of the whole tree and will nourish the ground for future generations. The book portrays a powerful message and Joy's father got it. He let go and died.

The next morning Joy stood gazing at the cold ocean and felt something hit her leg. She looked down and there was a giant, beautiful leaf. Joy picked it up and looked around and she too got the message. There were no trees on the beach, there were no leaves on the trees in late November, yet there was a giant leaf in her hand.

Joy knew this was her message, the leaf a messenger. Joy knew then she needed to do something with death and dying--that much was very clear. However, her path was not. That is why others were there to help her just as there are others to help those struggling for clarity with jobs and careers. Joy needed to acknowledge the sign and take a step forward to learn which career path she should take. And she did.

A life changing move forward for Joy. Scary? You bet! But once she started investigating, it was clear she was heading down the path to becoming whom she needed to be. It will work for you, too.

The secret is to be open to the messages and messengers. Be aware of those around you, be aware of what is around you, and listen to others and to your heart.

Now, indulge yourself a little. As you finish this chapter, treat yourself to one of these great recipes that offer comfort. Bon appetite!

Homemade Macaroni & Cheese (no blue box)

Kindergarten Sugar Cookies

Good Old Gingersnaps

Sally's Fancy Hot Chocolate

Macaroni & Cheese

1 – 7 oz. package of elbow macaroni
2 cups cottage cheese
1 cup sour cream
1 slightly beaten egg
¾ tsp. salt
¼ tsp. pepper
8 oz. sharp cheddar cheese

Cook elbow macaroni until nearly tender. Drain; blend with other ingredients. Turn into buttered baking dish. Sprinkle with Paprika. Bake 350° for 45 minutes.

Good Old Gingersnaps

2 cups flour	2 tsp. baking soda
1 tsp. ginger	1 tsp. cloves
1 tsp. cinnamon	¾ cup shortening
1 cup sugar	4 tbsp. molasses
1 egg	

Sift together flour, baking soda, ginger, cloves and cinnamon. Set aside. Cream shortening. Add sugar, egg and molasses. Beat well. Add flour mixture and beat until smooth. Mixture will be very stiff. Take a teaspoonful of mixture, roll into a ball, and then roll ball in sugar. Flatten with fork. Bake on greased cookie sheet for 10-12 minutes at 350°.

Kindergarten Sugar Cookies

4 c. flour   1 c shortening
1 ½ cup sugar   ½ tsp salt
1 tsp. soda   2 eggs well beaten
4 tsp. milk (may need more)
1 tsp vanilla

Mix flour and shortening like pie dough. Add sugar, salt and soda. Then add eggs, milk and vanilla.
Roll rather thick (about 1/8 or ¼ inch)
Cut in shapes; brush with milk and sugar.
Bake in 350 ?oven for 10-15 minutes. You can also frost when cool.
Makes about 5 dozen

Sally's Hot Chocolate

2/3 cup chocolate chips (semi sweet)
½ cup corn syrup
¼ cup plus 2 tbsp. water
1 tsp vanilla
2 cups whipping cream
8 cups milk
2 Tbsp chocolate syrup (Use a good brand)

Heat chocolate chips, corn syrup, and water over low heat; stirring until chocolate is melted and mixture is smooth. Stir in vanilla and chill. In chilled bowl, beat cream until stiff, gradually adding chocolate. Continue beating until mixture mounds when dropped from a spoon. Refrigerate. (this can be made ahead of time)
Just before serving, add chocolate syrup to milk and heat through but do not boil. Fill mugs ½ full with whipped cream mixture. Fill cups with milk; blend and serve.

Chapter 2

Assessments...The Appetizer

Now that you have worked through the pain and grief of loss, you are ready to whet your appetite. How do you do that? Let's start by perusing the appetizer menu of career development. You will learn how to assess yourself and make good choices about your career and try some great appetizers along the way.

Career development can be a long, tiring, stressful, and exciting process. It is an emotional roller coaster. It can be painfully long, with many difficulties. It can be discouraging. It can also be the most exciting and stimulating time in your life. We prefer to look at it as a time that is exciting and stimulating, when you re-introduce yourself to yourself. You get to look at your skills and maybe discover some talents you didn't know you had. You get to know the person you have been living with all these years.

In this chapter, you will learn about the tests, indicators, and assessments available to help you learn what skills and talents you have and how to develop them into a career direction.

You may already know what skills you have; you may even know what kind of job you are looking for. If you do, you are moving in the right direction. However, even if you have this information, you can still learn how to use it in the best way. You can do this by better understanding what you offer an employer.

Career assessment tests generally fall into two categories: personality and career or vocational. Clearly, the personality tests will not help you get a job, but they will help point you to what fits you when you look for a job. Personality tests will help predict how you are likely to perform the job and what environment works the best for you.

The fact is there are many web sites that offer free interactive tests that suggest career possibilities. Others can give you information about your personality "type" and how well suited you may be to individual career choices.

The controversy among career counselors and scholars is simply: 1) How reliable and accurate are these tests? 2) Should a job seeker trust any career-oriented assessment without a professional's interpretation and guidance?

We believe having a professional help you interpret the results of career assessments is a wise choice. Some on-line assessments can supplement a professional's help, not substitute for it.

Despite these concerns, free online career assessments can be helpful in ways that Richard Bolles summarizes best in his book, *What Color is Your Parachute?* "These assessments give you ideas you hadn't thought of and suggestions worth following up. The key is not to expect too much of the tests -- not to believe they will provide a magic answer that will guide the rest of your life and career."

Many of the following tests are free online and worth exploring. There are a lot more. This is just a sampling. Do more exploring for yourself.

The Keirsey Temperament Sorter

Author David Keirsey categorizes people by temperament, and it is possible through a better understanding of your temperament to gain more insight into the type of work that is best for you.

The Ennagram Institute

The Riso-Hudson Enneagram Type Indicator (RHETI) is another personality test, with the results grouping you among nine basic personality types.

ColorQuiz

Based on the famous work of Dr. Max Luscher, this simple free test takes five minutes. It is different from most personality tests in that all you do is click on colors.

The Classic IQ Test

Probably the best free IQ test available on the Web. This is our opinion.

Human Metrics â Jung Typology

A free test, based on the Myers-Briggs assessment.

Google Tests and Testing

If you find the above listed resources insufficient, take a look at Google's testing page.

There are many, many links to testing sites, some free and some not. Some are expensive. You decide what fits you best.

www.careerassessments.com

Interest inventory for all ages.

The Fairy Godmother Report on Test & Advice Sites

www.JobHuntersBible.com

What Color is My Parachute web site

www.careerkey.org

Career interest test online.

www.careerstrategy.org

Career advice as well as assessment suggestions.

www.myfuture.com

Work interest quiz.

www.2h.com/personality-tests.html

Personality tests on line.

Here is a list of the major online career assessment tools for job seekers: All listed assessments are interactive.

Assessment	Measures	Ease of Use	Detail of Results
Ansir's 3 Sides of Your Self Perception Profiling System This 168-question three-part self-perception test provides insight into your styles of thinking, working, and emoting. Cost: Free	Dominant personality styles in three realms: Thinking, Working and Emoting	Easy to use, but a bit time consuming (up to about 30 minutes).	Comprehensive results. More detailed results are available for a fee.
Big Five Personality Test Formerly called All About You, this 52-question test measures personality aspects that can be applied to careers. Cost: Free	Five fundamental dimensions of personality	Easy to use; takes 5-10 minutes	Fairly bare bones chart assessing Openness to New Experiences, Extraversion, Nervousness and others.
Campbell Interest and Skill Survey Online version of a well-known and reputable assessment containing 320 multiple-choice items. Cost: $18.00	Interests and Skills	Easy to use but time-consuming: 25-40 minutes.	Very comprehensive results, covering nearly 60 occupations and a comprehensive career planner to help you interpret your results and plan for your new career.
Career Assessment Test Cost: $6.95 for your level of satisfaction at work; $12.95 for your level of satisfaction at work plus a personalized assessment report (17 pages) and list of corresponding professions.	Your level of satisfaction at work.	50 questions; approximately 15 minutes.	17-page personalized report describing your basic qualities and traits at work, as well as a list of jobs that best suit you.
Career Competency Explorer from testingroom.com This 151-question assessment looks at strengths to see how they relate to day-to-day work performance. Cost: Free	Five career competency domains: Technical, Strategic, Innovation, Cooperation, and Influence.	Very easy interface; questions seem somewhat repetitious. Takes about 10-20 minutes. Registration required.	About 4 paragraphs of results covering the test-taker's preferred work environment, contributions to the organization and possible causes of stress.
Career Direct Personality ID Survey Cost: Personality ID Survey is free; full Career Direct Assessment is $80.	Personality	Assessment involves ranking 16 sets of 4 descriptive words as to how well they describe you.	Gives reasonably detailed results about personality type.

Assessment	Measures	Ease of Use	Detail of Results
Career Focus 2000 Interest Inventory This assessment's 180 inventory items about work tasks, drawn from 18 occupational fields that make up the U.S. work scene, help you identify possible career goals that match your strongest personal interests. Cost: Free	Level of interest in 18 occupational fields	Easy. Takes about 20-30 minutes.	A bar graph shows your level of interest in 18 occupational fields and tells how to further explore fields of highest interest.
Career Interest Inventory from Emode.com (Tickle) This test has you choose what you'd rather do among three choices for 44 questions. Cost: Free	"what you're naturally good at"	Easy. Takes about 5 minutes.	Results tell your top career area, with a one-paragraph description. A more detailed report ($4.95 with trial membership to Tickle.com) describes the 4 careers best suited to your interests.
Career Interest Inventory from testingroom.com This 180-question assessment is a measure of occupational and career interests. Cost: Free	Six fundamental categories of interests that capture most characteristics of people.	Very easy interface. Takes about 15 minutes. Registration required.	Two-paragraph report; more complete results available for $14.95. Free sample of full results available.
Career Liftoff This 240-question test uses activity-based questions to create a report with Holland/RIASEC codes. Cost: $14.95	Interests.	Very easy.	Detailed profile and narrative reports instantly available in PDF format.
Career link Inventory A 36-question assessment based on the premise that your self-estimates are a valid basis for career decision-making. Cost: Free	Interests, aptitudes, temperaments, physical capacities, preferred working conditions and desired length of time preparing for employment.	Easy	Tells which career clusters fit you and provides details about each cluster.

Assessment	Measures	Ease of Use	Detail of Results
Career Maze An on-line tool designed for people to find their future by increasing self-knowledge. Has you choose from among 2 sets of 82 characteristics. Cost: $19.95	How you see yourself and how you think others see you in terms of the 82 characteristics.	Very fast and easy to use.	Highly detailed, multi-page report tells your approach to goals, how you interact with the world around you, your natural pace, what you seek when given responsibility, plus career implications for these traits and jobs that fit your behavior pattern.
Career Personality Test from Emode.com This 38-question assessment gives results in terms of Myers-Briggs types. Cost: Free	Personality type.	Easy.	Results, expressed as a Myers-Briggs type, comprise about 3 paragraphs; a more detailed report ($9.95 with trial membership to Tickle.com) describes the best work environments for your type, and tells why you interact with colleagues the way you do -- and more.
Career Planner This test, based on the RIASEC system developed by Dr. John Holland, has 180 questions in which you either choose from two interest areas or answer true/false. Cost: $29.95 for 1-hour processing; $24.95 for 2-day processing; $19.95 for 5-day processing	The "fundamental nature of the careers that are good for you"	Easy. Takes 10-15 minutes.	Results, which are 10-11 pages long, are available at a Web site between an hour and five days after completing the test. Results include 30 to 100 careers matched to the test-taker's interests, values, and skill sets. Requires submission of significant personal information. Test is not an especially good value. Similar RIASEC-based tests -- which don't require submission of personal information -- are available free. Site makes overblown claims, such as: "You can use this knowledge to make career decisions for the rest of your life."

Assessment	Measures	Ease of Use	Detail of Results
Career Test by Career Fitter The 60-question assessment describes itself as a "hybrid." Questions very similar to those on a Myers-Briggs-type test. Cost: $9.95	Work personality, including strengths, weaknesses, styles, optimal environments, and other in-depth characteristics of the test-taker at work.	Easy. Takes 15-25 minutes.	10-page Career Report includes summary of test-taker, personality chart, career choices for test-taker, occupational factors, primary characteristics, and the test-taker at work, potential weaknesses, personality details, business points, communication method, ideal environment, team-building approach, management practice, and famous people like test-taker. You can view a sample report.
Career Values Scale from testingroom.com This 88-question assessment looks at values to see how they relate to the test-taker's world of work and help to identify areas of career satisfaction and dissatisfaction. Cost: Free	Ten work values: service orientation, team orientation, influence, creativity, independence, excitement, personal development, financial rewards, security and prestige.	Very easy interface; questions seem somewhat repetitious. Takes about 10-20 minutes Registration required.	Two-paragraph report; more complete results available for $8.95. Free sample of full results available.
Career Zone An extremely bare-bones, 3-question assessment. Cost: Free	Combinations of six broad interest areas known as RIASEC codes.	Ultra fast and easy	Very bare bones, but gives lists of occupations for each type. Test-takers will need to do more research on the RIASEC types.

Assessment	Measures	Ease of Use	Detail of Results
Carolyn Kalil's Personality Assessment (True Colors) True Colors is a personality system that has been around since 1979 and is modeled as a graphical presentation of both Keirsey's Temperament and the Meyers-Briggs Type Indicator. The assessment asks you to choose one of two ways to finish 36 statements. The results can help you define your skills and talents -- and possibly direct you to various career paths. Cost: Free	Personality	Easy. Takes just a few minutes.	Gives Web-based results in terms of one of four colors, explained with a one-paragraph description of your type. (You can also read about your second color.) More detailed results are e-mailed to the test-taker, and there are publications for sale that can offer even more insight.
Coach Compass® Assessment Cost: Free	Defines an appropriate starting point for career services and coaching delivery, thereby allowing for the targeted development of effective client strategies to ensure career success.	Easy. Choose 1 appropriate statement among 6 for 16 sets of statements.	A short report appears on-screen, and a very detailed report with graphs attached is e-mailed.

Assessment	Measures	Ease of Use	Detail of Results
FOCUS A comprehensive tool for career planning that's used in more than 1,000+ schools and career counseling centers nationwide. Cost: $18.95	Interests, skills, values, personality, educational preferences and leisure activities.	Has 9 phases that take up to 20 minutes each. More time can be spent by those who would like to explore several careers. At the beginning of FOCUS, you must choose which Web browser you're using and make a slight change in your preferences. The interface is easy.	Creates a profile of your interests, skills, values, personality, educational preferences and leisure activities, and enables you to investigate matching occupations and their related duties, education, skills needed, specific working conditions, required training, job outlook, current and expected earnings. You can view a sample report.
Future Proof Your Career This 84-question assessment helps the test-taker find fulfilling work and creates a personalized career strategy that works with the latest employment trends of the knowledge age. Cost: Free	Temperament type, dominant intelligences, dominant abilities, preferred learning style, test-taker's status as a knowledge worker and knowledge-age skills.	Easy. Registration required. Average completion time is around 10-12 minutes.	Comprehensive report covers test-taker's temperament type, three dominant intelligences, six dominant abilities, knowledge worker status, proficiency in the six key Knowledge Age Skills and preferred learning style. Interpretive book available for $27.
Hollands Self-Directed Search Online version of widely used and highly respected career assessment. Cost: $9.95	Interests, values, and skills	Takes 15-20 minutes.	8-10 page personalized report. You can view a sample report.
Jackson Vocational Interest Survey (JVIS) Developed to assist high school and college students and adults with educational and career planning, this test contains 289 pairs of job-related activities. Cost: $19.95	Vocational interests	Though quite long (takes 45 minutes.), the JVIS provides encouraging screens that tell your progress and give you a little pep talk.	Highly detailed report. A particular strength is the results' comparison of your similarity to college students in specific majors, thus suggesting possible majors for young people to consider. Detailed results. JVIS graphs your scores on 34 work roles and work styles.

Assessment	Measures	Ease of Use	Detail of Results
JASPER (Job Asset and Strengths Profiler) This 70-question assessment is related to the Myers-Briggs Type Indicator. Cost: Free for basic results; $59.95 for full report.	8 different job-related dimensions, including Work values, environment and work personality.	Entertaining graphical interface. Time-consuming (about 30 minutes), but test tells you percentage you've completed, and you can also save what you've done and go back to it.	Categorizes test-takers as one of the following: Thinker, Dynamo, Visionary, Motivator, Advocate, Organizer, Mentor, Achiever and Individualist. About a paragraph of detail, along with interesting graphics, on each of the 8 dimensions. Full report is available for $59.95.
Keirsey Temperament Sorter This 70-question assessment is related to the Myers-Briggs Type Indicator. Cost: Free	Personality	Easy to use, but a little time consuming. Registration required.	Results, in the form of partial Myers-Briggs Types, give descriptions of the types. More detailed report available for $14.95.
Live Career This 100-question assessment identifies your career interests and then tells you what jobs are out there for you. Free for basic results.	Basic interests	Easy. Takes 25 minutes. You can stop and go back to the test later. You also have the opportunity to review your answers before submitting them.	Gives basic interest scores based on RIASEC scales, along with matching job clusters and links to Monster's job search.
MAPP (Motivational Appraisal of Personal Potential) Career Analysis This test has 71 triads of three statements. You must select the statement you MOST agree with and the statement you LEAST agree with, leaving one blank. Cost: Free for very minimal report; detailed reports start at $19.95	Interest in job contents, temperament for the job, aptitude for the job, people, things, data, reasoning, mathematical capacity, language capacity.	Registration required; fairly easy to use, but requires some thought.	Free results are essentially a teaser to encourage purchase of paid results; however, free MAPP match features that compare your results with 5 chosen jobs is helpful.

Assessment	Measures	Ease of Use	Detail of Results
Maze master This 6-part assessment is geared to high school and college students. Cost: Free	Interests, skills, and values.	Fairly easy; takes about 30 minutes. Registration required. Registration is set up for Canadians, but others can use it.	Rather than interpretive results, the report is a compilation of the Interests, Skills, and Values, the test-taker has chosen, along with Goals, Next Steps, and Action Plan. Links provide additional information on careers suggested by the Interest results.
Obik Explorer (high school and younger college students) Obik Pathfinder (older college students and recent grads) Obik Discovery for Career Transitioners Offers 505 short questions, 202 of which relate to what interests you, 72 of which relate to what you are good at and 231 of which relate to who you are. Cost: $25 for Explorer; $30 for Pathfinder	Interests, skills, and personality traits, as well as suitability of college majors and careers.	n/a	n/a
Personality Index from testingroom.com This 90-question assessment examines key personality features that influence your approach to tasks, interaction with people and the activities you enjoy. Cost: Free	17 traits: ambition, initiative, flexibility, energy, leadership, concern for others, teamwork, outgoing, democratic, innovation, analytic thinking, persistence, dependability, attention to detail, rule-following, self-control and stress tolerance.	Very easy interface; questions seem somewhat repetitious. Takes about 10-20 minutes. Registration required.	Two-paragraph report describes two key features of your personal style; full report with an additional 20 traits available for $14.95. Free sample of full results available.

A Taste for Work

Assessment	Measures	Ease of Use	Detail of Results
Princeton Review Career Quiz This 24-question quiz is a summary version of Birkman Method, designed to give you a taste of the full tool. Cost: Free	Interests and work style	Very fast and easy	Gives results in terms of colors, one for interests and one for work style. About a paragraph of detail for each. If you register, you can also get a list of careers -- with detailed information -- that match your "colors."
Right Job, Wrong Job from Emode.com This 41-question assessment helps you determine your "career personality" and if you're in the right job. Cost: Free	Career personality.	Easy.	Results are about 3 paragraphs; more detailed report ($14.95 with trial membership to Tickle.com) lists the right job that is a statistical match for your personality and the wrong job that is a statistical disaster for your personality.
Riso-Hudson Enneagram Type Indicator (RHETI) SAMPLE This 38-question assessment, a sample of the full RHETI which has 144 questions, looks at personality types. Cost: Free	Personality	Easy to use. Takes 5-10 minutes.	Fairly good description of 1 of 9 types
Strengths Finder Profile This well-researched instrument asks you to choose to what degree either of a set of paired statements applies to you. Cost: "Free" with the purchase of $27 book, Now, Discover Your Strengths, which provides an access code.	Areas in which you have the greatest potential for strength.	Easy. Takes about 25 minutes. Warning! There's a 20-second limit for answering each question before it vanishes from the screen.	Online results consist of a good sized paragraph describing your five most dominant themes of talent and your signature themes. Accompanying book provides more detail on each theme.
The Career Key 66-question test, providing another variation on Holland codes. Cost: $7.95	Interests, skills, values, self-image	Easy to use. Takes 10 minutes.	Results are in the form of Holland Codes with lists of jobs that fit each code provided; links to Occupational Outlook Handbook for more info about each career.

Assessment	Measures	Ease of Use	Detail of Results
Type Focus Personality Type Profile Quick and easy 66-question assessment that tells your Myers-Briggs type and offers a bit of career direction. Cost: Free	Personality	Easy to use. A little faster than the Kiersey/about 8 minutes	Results are in the form of Myers-Briggs Personality types; somewhat detailed, but not a large amount of career info; more detailed results (7 reports) available for $14.95
What's the Right Job for You? Cost: $6.95	Identifies the jobs that best match your temperament, lifestyle and attitude toward others.	50 questions and requires around 12 to 15 minutes.	20-page personalized report describing your basic qualities and traits at work, as well as a list of jobs that best suit you.
Work Preference Inventory This 24-question forced-choice assessment that tells your work style. Based on the premise that the process of values clarification is very important in career planning. Cost: Free	Values	Quick and easy; interactivity depends on having a Java-enabled browser	Results are in a chart with very brief descriptions of work style; tests with more detailed results available for a fee.

And more:

    Search engine: Google - personality tests

    Search engine: overture - personality tests

    Search engine: Excite - personality tests

    Search engine: Webcrawler - personalitytests

    Here are a couple of "Values Inventory" links Some believe you get a better idea of what work you like by determining what you value most.

    Search engine: Google - Values Inventories

    Search engine: Overture - Values Inventories

    Search engine: Excite - Values Inventories

    Search engine: Webcrawler - Values Inventories

    "Attitude Test" links...Some employment professionals believe you get a better picture of what drives your behavior by knowing what your attitude is.

Search engine: Google - Attitude Tests

Search engine: Excite - Attitude Tests

Search engine: Webcrawler - Attitude Tests

And finally:

Job Analysis/Classification & Personality Research

Download Personality Profile Software

New Mental Health / Clinical Psychology Web Site!

Remember, this is a continually evolving index. Do your own searching and find what fits you best. This is a time in your life for exploring.

We also have some very simple exercises that each of us has tried with success over the years. They are simple, quick, easy to use, and practical. However, most importantly, if you write it down, it becomes real. Get yourself some paper and a pencil with a good eraser. Take the time to write; it works.

1. What I Hated About My Jobs

Directions: In column one, write down everything you hate about the job you had or the career that does not fulfill you anymore. Write about the people you worked with, and the kind of building you worked in. Write whatever you want and as much as you want, but write it all out. In the other column, write the opposite of everything you hate. If you hate it, you like or love the opposite. This column is about what you love, love, love about the job. When you finish--and it could take a while--, you will have your ideal job in the second column.

2. Every job I Have Ever Had

Directions: Fill each category for *every* job you have ever had.

After you have completed each category for every job, write a job description about what you learned, what you liked about the job, and the value you brought to the position.

Page 2: Where to Look: List where you would find the jobs for that description. What industries are you interested in? Profit or not for profit? Product or service? Don't worry about identifying employers' right now; focus on the job.

3. Dare to Step Out!

Directions: What activities would you do or participate in if you weren't concerned about whether or not you were good at what you were doing? List them.

4. What I Want To Be When I Grow Up

Directions: Sit in a comfortable quiet place where you will not be disturbed for at least 30 minutes. Close your eyes and remember when you were a child.

As a child, we imagine ourselves as all kinds of interesting people, both real and imaginary. When I was six, I imagined myself as Superman. I used to wrap a sheet around my neck and jump off our chicken coop roof yelling, "I am super, duper, pooper man." I remember loving that jump and imagining I could fly.

Nobody expects you to dream being Superman or jump off chicken coops, but maybe you dreamed of being a fire fighter, a doctor, a farmer, a teacher, or an inventor. What was it about that occupation that attracted you? Write the occupation in the first column.

Now think, what about that job did you like? If you wanted to be a fire fighter, did you like thinking of the danger of fighting a fire? Was it the excitement of facing the unexpected? Did you dream of saving people? Did you see fire fighters as integral to building a safer community?

There was something that drew you to the occupation, a something that attracted you; now is the time to remember and dream it up.

Fill in column two with everything you liked about that job/activity/work.

In column three, look at what you've written about the jobs and why you liked them. Write a job description using the characteristics you loved as a child.

Nobody will see this but you. Take your time, you have all the answers. Give yourself a chance to think, record and answer yourself. Remember, writing it down makes it real.

4. Where Do I Thrive?

Directions: Think about the environment and culture you want in your next job. What environment do you need to nurture or feed yourself to perform at your best? This is another imagination exercise. Sit in a comfortable quiet place where you will not be disturbed for at least 30 minutes. Close your eyes and think of everything you can think of that will make your work environment perfect. Now visualize it. It can be anything from the color of the carpet to how many windows you look out to what food is in the vending machines. Do you want to work on a team or are you better working alone? Describe the place, the culture, the kind of people you want to work with, what would your boss be like? Write it all down.

When you finish you will see the kind of culture and work environment where you will perform at your best. This is valuable information as you interview and see the variety of cultures that are out there.

5. How Well Do You Know Me?

Directions: Interview eight people--friends, family, co-workers, and former bosses. People who know you well and care about you. Look for people who have your best interests at heart as well as those who can be candid.

Listen to their answers and record them. Do not argue, simply record and digest. You may ask what their reasoning is or what they base their opinion on, but you may not defend yourself or argue with them, even if you don't agree. Ask the following three questions and record what they say.

- What do you think my greatest strengths are when I communicate with others?
- What do you think my greatest weaknesses are?
- What single gesture or habit betrays me and makes me seem unconfident?

Remember: We discover our vocations bit by bit, through the process of living and working and by paying attention to what draws us, moves us, and brings us more alive. In this exercise, learning to pay attention to our likes, dislikes, and yearnings is as essential a life skill as any other that we may ever hone. We must respect the gravity of what we love, and learn to accept and yield to the irresistible pull.

Review each sheet. Do you see a trend? Do you need an action plan to begin correcting how others see you? Maybe you need an action plan to decide how to develop your strengths? Now is the time to write the plan.

6. What Type of Work Attracts You?

Directions: Cut out job ads or any news articles about a specific field of employment that interests you. Put each of them in a file. Do not be deterred by any training requirements. A pattern will emerge.

7. Follow Your Lifeline: Uncovering Hidden Career Interests

Directions: Write down your significant achievements/dreams along the way. Once you have completed this exercise, review your record. Do this for your life up to the present. What is important about each achievement? Try to remember what it was like as you were living each achievement. Write your thoughts and feelings about each achievement.

8. Career Detective

Directions: When you work your way through career transition exercises, you gain a better idea of what interests you, but you may know very little about the type of work and the people who do it. It is time to set up informational interviews. You need to determine if this is the type of work you'd enjoy doing. Think about what you want to learn and record your questions. Examples of the types of questions you may want to ask:

- How did you get into this line of work? What type of training or expertise is required?
- Are you aware of anyone who works in this field without the traditional training? If so, what experience does he have?
- What do you like/dislike about your job?
- What is your primary daily task? Describe a typical day.
- How do you see someone with my experience fitting in? Would you review my resume and tell me if it properly targets this industry?

9. Job Shadowing

Directions: Job shadowing is a worthwhile activity to consider when researching a career area. A job shadow is an opportunity for you to spend a few hours going to the actual worksite and observing what occurs in a typical day. Usually a worker has the assignment of mentoring you. Your mentor will orient you and may be available to answer questions. Record your observations. What did you learn?

After you have taken your assessments and discussed your results with an expert, the next step is to explore your options. Remove your blinders and clearly review your interests, think about all the answers to your questions, think of your dreams. This may require some creativity and courage. We are asking you to look where you may have never looked before. A new world is waiting for you, be open to accept it.

After all this work, are you hungry? Try these tasty appetizers!

Then get ready for the next course -- soup!

Julie's Cranberry Glazed Baked Brie

Fancy Pinwheels

Sarah's No Bean Dip

Teri's Spinach Dip

Julie's Cranberry Glazed Baked Brie

3 c fresh cranberries (or 2 c dried)	¾ c brown sugar
1/3 c dried currants	1/3 c water
1/8 tsp. ground allspice	1/8 tsp. cardamom
1/8 tsp. ginger	1/8 tsp. cloves
½ c chopped pecans	2.2 lbs. Brie Cheese (8" diameter)

(2) Sheets of Puff Pastry (thawed)

Make marmalade by combining cranberries, brown sugar, currants, water and spices. Cook over medium heat until berries pop; stir frequently (about 5 minutes). Cool to room temperature. (This can be prepared up to 3 days ahead of serving).

Using a sharp knife, cut a circle in top rind of cheese leaving 1/2" border. Remove center circle.

Line cookie sheet with foil. Place thawed puff pastry on foil; place cheese round on top. Sprinkle pecans on top of cheese; pour marmalade on top; lightly spreading. Place 2nd puff pastry sheet on top and pinch sides together. With sharp knife make 2 slits on top. Bake at 400 for 20 minutes.

Serve with sliced pears, grapes, crackers and apples.

Fancy Pinwheels

Flour Tortilla Shells (fresh)
6 oz. can black olives (diced)
4 oz. green olives (diced)
Small jar pimento (diced)
8 oz. cream cheese (room temperature)

Combine ingredients and spread on tortilla shells. Roll tortilla; jelly roll like. Using a sharp knife, slice into ¼ to 1/2" rounds. Easy and delicious.

Sarah's No Bean Dip

8 oz. cream cheese
1 can Hormel Chili (no beans)
8 oz. Monterey Jack Cheese
Combine ingredients and place in microwave safe dish. Cover with plastic wrap. Microwave on high 5-7 minutes.
Serve warm with tortilla chips.

Teri's Spinach Dip

1-cup sour cream

1-cup Hellman's mayonnaise

1 package frozen chopped spinach

6 green onions, chopped

1 package Knorr's vegetable soup mix

1 can water chestnuts, chopped

1 loaf of Hawaiian Bread

Prepare frozen spinach according to package directions, drain, and squeeze until very dry. Then mix with the rest of the ingredients. Chill over night.

Before serving, scoop out the inside of the bread loaf and fill with the spinach dip. Break the extra bread into pieces and place around the loaf for dipping.

Chapter 3

Resumes

Soup - Not - Salad...

There are some good reasons to start-off a great meal with soup. A tasty soup can introduce the theme of a meal. Egg drop or Won ton soup really gets you ready for a delicious Asian meal. Minestrone or Pasta Fagioli soup can prime your taste buds for lasagna. Before a meal, soup prepares you for what is coming next.

On the other hand, some people like to start with a salad. Salads are delicious, but sometimes a salad takes over the meal because there are so many different tastes and textures of food that go into it.

Starting your meal with soup allows you to wake-up your taste buds and at the same time prepares you for a great meal.

So, let's stick with soup as our main appetizer for the sake of this discussion. Your resume is as the **Soup** of your job search. The flavor of your resume introduces you to the prospective employer and clearly identifies what you bring to the table. The purpose of your resume is an introduction to contacts and to get you job interviews.

Let's look at it in terms of a soup label or reading over a menu. There you are in a restaurant poring over the menu or at your local grocery store standing in the soup aisle. What is it that draws your attention to a particular soup? Often, it is the picture in the menu or on the label. What are we all trained to do now when it comes to food choices? Look at the ingredients and nutrition facts! We are all conditioned to look for these facts and note the number of calories, amount of fat and salt. However, take note, the whole recipe for the soup is not on the label; and generally, not all the ingredients are listed on a menu!

Let's look at your resume in the same terms. Design your resume with the same intention as a soup label or a menu item; the appearance will draw the prospective employer to it. What will draw attention? No, you don't want a picture…but you want your resume to have an easy-to-read, attractive, compelling, professional appearance. Fill it with words that describe your abilities using key terms common to your industry.

Your resume will need to survive the screening process. Often hiring screeners need to review hundreds, maybe even thousands, of resumes. What is going to make your resume stand out from all the rest?

Once a prospective employer decides to pick your resume, what is going make him/her "look for the nutrition facts and ingredients" and eventually invite you in for an interview? In addition to an attractive appearance and healthy words describing your abilities, your resume needs to highlight your accomplishments effectively. Spice up your resume with result-oriented accomplishments that will make the employer know that you will be profitable to his company. Your resume will entice the employer to invite you in for the interview to *get your whole dish* and he/she can learn how you will enhance his/her entire company's menu.

This chapter is about the soup course of your job search….your resume!

There are three generally accepted resume formats – **Chronological, Functional, or Combination.** All three formats should be no more than two pages, highlight your abilities and accomplishments, and be easy to read. It is professionally acceptable to use more than one format for your resume.

• Chronological

A chronological resume is reminiscent of a broth-based soup. You know what you are looking at right from the beginning. It is straightforward and reliable, comparable to a good old fashioned, chicken noodle soup. It is the most common; and that can be comforting. This type of resume presents information in a timeline approach: the most recent work experience followed by education and professional development information. This resume works well if you are planning to stay in the same industry and job title. Its format stresses the positions you have held and the companies where you have worked. The chronological style is appropriate for people who can show a stable work history with no substantial gaps between jobs.

- ## Functional

A functional resume allows you to focus on your relevant skills and accomplishments without matching that information to a specific title and company. This format is a little different; it plays down your work history and emphasizes your skills and accomplishments. It works well for people entering the job market for the first time or those re-entering the workforce. A functional resume also suits job seekers who are transitioning to a new career and want to emphasize specific transferable skills. A functional resume is like a bowl of taco soup. It highlights the flavor of a good Mexican meal.

- ## Combination

A combination resume brings together the best of the chronological and functional formats. The Key Accomplishment section allows you to shine a spotlight on results you want an employer to see. These results can be from current or former jobs or from volunteer activities. This type of resume works well for more mature workers as well as those changing industries. The Key Accomplishment section easily allows you to indicate your worth to the employer. (Remember the employer is looking at profitability and the bottom line.) What does an employer need to know? He needs to know that you are going to help make money for the company in some way…something that will help pump up the bottom-line.

Choosing a format for your resume is like snapping a picture for a soup label or menu.

Dress it UP!

You have chosen your format. Now you have to start dressing it up to get the reader really interested! Make it easy for the employer to know what type of job you are seeking. No lengthy objective statements; all they say is you are looking for a job. The reader already knows that because you have a resume. Instead, indicate your job title or titles (you can have more than one, but no more than two or three) in the same size font as your name. Yes, nice and big. Remember, this is helping you be picked off the shelf or out of the menu. Let the reader know what you want.

Example:

GLOBAL SALES MANAGER
or
ACCOUNTING/AUDITING PROFESSIONAL

It is your responsibility to define your job title or titles. You cannot expect a prospective employer to identify it/them for you. There is a great website to help you pin it down. ONET also known as the *Dictionary of Occupational Titles Online*. Here is the link: http://online.onetcenter.org/

On the opening page, click on Find Occupations link, this will take you to a page where you can use keywords to search for your job title. The keyword search gives you a list of job titles; as you click on each title, you will find information regarding tasks, knowledge, skills, abilities, and specific work activities.

By using this site for research, you will be able to *name* yourself, which will allow the employer to see what you are bringing to the table.

Next up is your summary statement. A summary statement is directly under your job title(s). Your statement should be a brief description (three to five lines). It gives the reader insight into who you are (characteristics) and what strengths you will bring to the job. Remember; these are descriptors, not complete sentences. You do not want it to read like an essay (no pronouns). You want to have a BLUE RIBBON statement, too. A BLUE RIBBON statement is something that differentiates you from everyone else.

The major points that should be included in your summary statement are:

1. Characteristics that are important to you and the job you want.
2. Specific strengths
3. A BLUE RIBBON statement.

The Summary Statement differs from an objective. An objective says what you want from the employer. It puts you in a very narrow job opportunity situation, in other words, it is limiting. That is not what you want.

It is also important to know the jargon of your industry and the company you are addressing. There can be a problem with semantics;

meaning you may call what you do one name and the employer may call it something different. Here is where researching this company is important. Reading about the company in several places will give you a feel for their language and get you on the same page as your perspective employer.

A summary statement should make the reader want to know more about you. Keep in mind, probably no one is going to read your *entire* resume. The employer or human resources representative may actually read 1/3 of your resume and visually scan the rest. Make this first piece easy to read and compelling enough to make the reader interested in scanning the rest.

Here are some examples:

- A. "A comprehensive record of sales and management in the automotive industry. Proven ability to generate new sales growth up to $80 million annually and evaluate sales organizations to effectively target new customers and win challenging accounts. Excellent interpersonal and communication skills. Knowledgeable and pro-active with high energy and integrity."

- B. "Dependable and detail-oriented accounting and auditing professional. Successful in meeting deadlines and working under pressure. Saved over $1.5 million by finding and eliminating accounting errors. Able to multi-task; organized and focused. Specific expertise helping organizations reach maximum potential with sound accounting practices."

Spice it UP!

The resume gets noticed when it emphasizes how you are going to help the prospective employer make money. Like it or not, money is what drives business whether you are working for a profit corporation or a nonprofit organization. Now you must spice up your resume by indicating how you have positively affected the bottom line in former positions. If you did it before, you will do it again. This will separate you from the rest of the pack.

For example, a good rule is to indicate in your resume that you are worth 3 to 5 times your salary. If you want to make $50,000 somewhere in your bullet points you need to demonstrate how you helped former companies make $150,000 to $250,000. It does not have to be pure profit; the figure can be soft savings, too. Determine this number by how you saved time (days, months), resources (how much), managed costs in programs (how much), or maintained a budget (how big). At first, that $50,000 might sound like a lot of money; but in reality when you start reviewing your accomplishments, you will see that you helped former employers make a lot more money than you thought. And your salary was only $50,000!

To help you start thinking about accomplishments, review some of your prior performance evaluations. This can be a good place to start jogging your memory. Take a look at the assessments chapter; you started writing about them there.

Further, here is a list of questions to help you remember what you accomplished. These questions probe to help you start thinking about what you have achieved in former positions.

In a previous job did you:

- Achieve more without utilizing increased resources?
- Achieve the same result but reduced utilization of resources?
- Achieve improved operations or relations?
- Achieve a goal for the first time?
- Achieve resolution of problems or conflicts with little or no negative effect?

The key is to clearly, indicate how you affected the bottom-line. Did you help the company make money? Your bullet points are the place to shout about it.

Now you are really beginning to get yourself noticed. Go a step further.
Make it easy for the employer to see what you can do!

Whenever possible start your statements with the result, followed by the action you engaged in to gain the result. As someone reviews your resume, the 'results-oriented' word at the beginning of the statement attracts him. The following is a list of results-oriented words and phrases frequently mentioned on resumes. Each one requires a quantitative or qualitative measure to make it valid. Resume reviewers love to see numbers. Whenever possible, indicate your result with a number, dollar amount, or percentage. It is something solid to hang your achievement on.

- Improved or increased productivity by…
- Increased profits by……….

- Reduced costs by..........
- Expanded markets..........
- Increased market share by.........
- Reduced shrinkage/improved quality..............
- Decreased down time by.........
- Lowered number/frequency of.........
- Reduced time by.............
- Created/introduced new technological process.......
- Created new/improved administrative process.........
- Reduced training time by.........
- Enlarged specific skill........
- Created/implemented specific controls/measures of performance....
- Created new plans.......
- Implemented/directed a program.........
- Solved problems, identified/defined solutions..........
- Foresaw a need and............

Remember; the goal is to have someone so excited by your resume they will want to meet you in person. WOW them with your incredible accomplishments. Whet their appetite and make them HUNGRY to meet you!

Sprinkle your resume liberally with tasty morsels of words that make them want more of you.

Here are lists of words that add power and link your phrases together for effective statements.

LINKING PHRASES	ADJECTIVES	NOUNS
• Extensive experience	• Detail oriented	• Communicator
• Progressive experience	• Motivated	• Organizer
• Broad range experience	• Creative	• Problem solver
• Comprehensive experience	• Analytical	• Decision maker
• Substantial experience	• Results oriented	• Change agent
• Increasing responsibility	• Driven	• Business developer
• Major strengths are	• Enthusiastic	• Designer
• Key strengths include	• Multi-faceted	• Facilitator
• Areas of expertise	• Adaptable	• Coach
• Outstanding record in	• Flexible	• Mentor
• Outstanding results	• Multi-tasking	• Visionary
• Worked effectively with	• Self-starting	• Manager
• Highly successful record of	• Diverse	• Executive
• Strong background in	• Trustworthy	• Advocate
• Capable of	• Dedicated	• Consultant
• Thoroughly familiar with	• Loyal	• Professional
• A proven record of	• Reliable	• Team leader
• Successful accomplishments in	• Determined	• Team player
• Proven executive	• Competent	• Team member
• Outstanding track record	• Innovative	• Key member
• With ability to	• Supportive	• Team builder
	• Proactive	• Time manager
	• Consultative	• Writer
	• Energetic	• Presenter
	• Versatile	• Leader
	• Decisive	• Negotiator
	• Tenacious	• Collaborator
	• Positive	• Trainer
	• Skilled	• Teacher
	• Bottom line oriented	• Administrator
	• Empowering	• Motivator
	• Dynamic	
	• Collaborative	

ACTION WORDS

Accelerated	Devised	Made	Revived
Accomplished	Directed	Maintained	Saved
Achieved	Discovered	Managed	Scheduled
Acquired	Discharged	Marketed	Secured
Adapted	Distributed	Mediated	Selected
Addressed	Documented	Minimized	Served
Administered	Doubled	Mobilized	Settled
Advanced	Earned	Modernized	Shaped
Advised	Edited	Modified	Showed
Allocated	Eliminated	Monitored	Simplified
Analyzed	Employed	Motivated	Sold
Anticipated	Enforced	Negotiated	Solved
Applied	Established	Obtained	Specified
Appointed	Estimated	Operated	Sponsored
Approved	Evaluated	Ordered	Staffed
Arranged	Examined	Organized	Standardized
Assessed	Exceeded	Originated	Started
Attained	Executed	Overcame	Stimulated
Audited	Exercised	Overhauled	Streamlined
Augmented	Expanded	Participated	Strengthened
Broadened	Expedited	Performed	Stretched
Budgeted	Extended	Pinpointed	Structured
Built	Financed	Planned	Studied
Calculated	Forecasted	Prepared	Supervised
Centralized	Formed	Presented	Supported
Chaired	Found	Prevented	Surpassed
Collaborated	Founded	Prioritized	Surveyed
Combined	Fulfilled	Procured	Sustained
Composed	Generated	Produced	Tailored
Completed	Guided	Promoted	Taught
Conceived	Halved	Proposed	Terminated
Concluded	Headed	Programmed	Tested
Condensed	Helped	Projected	Traded
Conducted	Hired	Proved	Trained
Consolidated	Identified	Published	Transacted
Constructed	Implemented	Realized	Transformed
Consulted	Improved	Recommended	Translated
Contracted	Increased	Reconciled	Trimmed
Contributed	Influenced	Recruited	Tripled
Controlled	Initiated	Reduced	Uncovered
Converted	Innovated	Reestablished	Undertook
Coordinated	Inspected	Regulated	Unified
Corrected	Installed	Reinforced	Used
Created	Instituted	Re-negotiated	Utilized
Cut	Instructed	Reorganized	Verified
Decentralized	Integrated	Reported	Widened
Decreased	Introduced	Represented	Withdrew
Defined	Invented	Researched	Won
Delivered	Investigated	Reshaped	Worked
Demonstrated	Launched	Resolved	Wrote
Designed	Led	Restored	
Determined	Liquidated	Reviewed	
Developed	Located	Revised	

Tidbits for extra flavor!

A resume should:

- Be concise
- Have lots of white space
- Be easy to read
- Be attractive in appearance
- Include professional keywords
- Be limited to 1 to 2 pages of information
- Have complete contact information at the top of every page
- List duties and achievements
- Include brief, easy to read statements
- Contain clear and concise education/training information

A resume should not:

- Be on colored paper as it is too dark to be copied easily.
- Be printed on an ink jet printer, laser recommended, it makes a finer copy.
- Be over two pages. No one will read more than two pages.
- Have graphics, fancy borders, designs or pictures
- Be stapled or in folders or binders. Staples, clips, binders tend to jam a system.
- Have misspelled words
- Have personal information regarding spouse, children, height, and weight
- Present information in a disorganized fashion
- Have long paragraphs of information. Concise bullet points are easier to read.
- Be puffed up with trivia. Don't waste the reader's time.
- Have a lengthy education section with meaningless courses. Lengthy section often signals you don't have a degree.

A big question today is whether you should include your street address on your resume. Some people think leaving it off protects your privacy. Eliminating your address from your resume may raise a concern. Are you hiding something? Are you homeless?

Just using a post office box number may raise a question as well. Once again, what are you trying to hide? Consider that your address is rather easy for most people to find anyway. Don't raise a red flag unnecessarily.

If you are concerned about including your street address, at least include your city, state, and zip code. This gives the prospective employer an indication that you have a place to live and you are just protecting your privacy.

On the other hand, some human resource people will not call you for an interview if your address is 40 miles away. They may assume your commute is too long. You decide – there is no right or wrong answer.

When you have a first draft of your resume, ask for feedback from people in your field. Ask as many people as you like. But…..do not argue with their criticism! You should not take any advice you do not agree with. Consider valid suggestions.

There is power in a resume…

There are times when seeing your resume in written form can change how you feel about yourself. Looking at your accomplishments in black and white can boost your morale.

There was a client named Joe who had experienced some serious difficulties in his life due in part to his environment and some unfortunate decisions he made. In reality, at first glance, one would have considered Joe an unsavory character. However, when you spoke to him his genuine friendliness and gratitude for help was evident.

Joe came to an employment center on a dreary, cold November day. The center was serving hot soup for lunch, and Joe had walked several miles to the center for the soup and some help with his resume. He arrived just as the center was closing for the day. Joe was greeted and a big smile broke out on his weary face. He said: "I knew you would be here and welcome me in; any soup left?" Fortunately, there was enough for a hearty serving for him.

Joe made himself comfortable chatting and enjoying the soup, then he pulled a wadded up paper from his back pocket. The paper had obviously been in his pocket for some time. Smiling, he unfolded the paper and revealed the resume that someone in the center had prepared for him at least five years earlier.

That may not seem surprising until you consider that Joe had spent time in prison and had moved around countless times. Joe had been carrying that piece of paper with him all of those years. He said that he would pull it out of his pocket from time to time to remind himself that there were times when he made good decisions and had accomplished something worthwhile. At the time of his visit to the center, he wanted to update his resume so he could improve his life by finding a new job.

Though most of us do not have the difficulties that Joe has faced, we all question our value from time to time. A little nourishing soup and a good review of your resume will remind you of your unique worth and what you have to offer an employer.

MICHAEL C. DOUGLAS
555 N. Hiawatha Avenue Anywhere, IL 60000
(630) 555-1234
Michael_douglas@yahoo.com

VICE PRESIDENT / EQUITY INVESTMENT

A comprehensive record of success managing institutional and high-net worth accounts. Gained 40% return on investments. Excellent communication and interpersonal skills. Successful track record with above-market investment performance. Proven success in bringing in new business and retaining existing clients.

> Use bullet points to indicate how you affected the bottom-line by 3 to 5 times your salary!

EMPLOYMENT HISTORY

Johnson Bank, Chicago, IL (June 2003 – Present)
Vice President

- Minimized market risk over 50% and allowed above market returns by creating and implementing equity investment process in two product portfolios
- Developed and created the marketing material used for presentation of the investment process which helped bank meet 2008 AUM goal
- Increased client loyalty by establishing strong relationship of trust, which allowed 100% client retention maintaining $10 million of business.
- Increased annual investments by over 20% by establishing client investment expectations, designing and implementing use of investment Policy Statement

MarWay Bank, Chicago, IL (September 2000 - June 2003)
Investment Officer

- Managed high net worth client investment portfolios using quantitative and fundamental modeling factors
- Implemented investment education program which improved investment skills of portfolio managers; developed countrywide continuing education program
- Assigned by Chief Portfolio Manager to sit on Career Development Committee to resolve concerns and analyze portfolio manager operations
- Co-authored document which recommended changes to corporate investment policy and operations

MetLife Insurance Company, Chicago, IL (August 1996 – September 2000)
Investment Analyst

- Improved company's operating and revenue capacity with management oversight of money allocation for $8 billion portfolio
- Analyzed the valuation and modeled the business plan of various companies which allowed the company to make prudent investment acquisitions

EDUCATION

Bachelor of Science Degree – Business Management, Finance Emphasis
Marriott School of Management, Brigham Young University, Provo, UT

MICHAEL C. DOUGLAS
555 N. Hiawatha Avenue
Anywhere, IL 60000
(630) 555-1234
Michael_douglas@yahoo.com

MARKETING PROFESSIONAL - SALES MANAGER

A comprehensive and successful record of marketing, sales management, design, and engineering with an emphasis on customer satisfaction and service. Responsible for $13 million out of $40 million overall revenue. Extensively marketed capital equipment in the graphic arts and manufactured materials industries.

RELEVANT SKILLS & ACCOMPLISHMENTS

Marketing/Product Development/Management

- Reduced errors by sales staff 75% by developing and implementing comprehensive standardized quotations
- Designed multi-color sales literature and marketing materials
- Managed three national trade show exhibits staying within budget guidelines
- Increased sales 12% annually through effective cold calling and marketing of four new product lines
- Designed and implemented computer based pricing system to eliminate calculation errors
- Supervised development and printing of company's first catalog of standard products
- Enhanced revenue $1.5 million within two years by researching markets and identifying new growth product lines
- Conducted market feasibility studies and developed promotional sales packages and tools

> Use bullet points to indicate how you affected the bottom-line by 3 to 5 times your salary!

Direct Sales - Capital Equipment/Capital Materials

- Effectively called on established key accounts and developed new customers
- Met or exceeded sales goals regularly by an average of 36%
- Provided solutions to customers needs and problems which resulted in business increase of 100%
- Resolved service issues that convinced customers to buy exclusively from company

MICHAEL C. DOUGLAS - (630) 555-1234   Page Two

EMPLOYMENT HISTORY

Rockwell International Graphic Systems, Downers Grove, IL
(Sales Manager, Inside Sales Representative) 1995-present

Chicago Tribune Company, Chicago, IL
(Product Manager) 1992-1995

TRAINING & AWARDS

American Management Association - Salesman of the Year@ 2000 and 2004

Karrass Effective Negotiations@

Zig Ziglar I Can@

Kaizen Competitive Success@

Proficient in Microsoft Office and Internet Research

EDUCATION

Bachelor of Science Degree-Business Management
University of Illinois – Chicago, IL

MICHAEL C. DOUGLAS

555 N. Hiawatha Avenue (630) 555-1234
Anywhere, IL 60000 Michael_douglas@yahoo.com

SENIOR FINANCIAL EXECUTIVE / CONTROLLER

A comprehensive and successful record of financial management and accounting with extensive experie.02nce in financial reporting, analysis, operations, taxation, treasury management and accounting systems. Reduced accounting errors by 20% saving over $1.5 million annually. Excellent leadership and team building skills; a proactive manager.

Key Accomplishments

> Use bullet points to indicate how you affected the bottom-line by 3 to 5 times your salary!

- Increased net operating income 75% over a period of 3 years for an acquisition of a portfolio of 40 commercial properties through active involvement in leasing strategies, capital improvement decisions and oversight of ongoing property expenses.

- Decreased physical inventory variances by 90% and achieved substantial improvements in job cost variance analysis through closely coordinating the integration of a new cost accounting system with the company's manufacturing system.

- Reduced outside audit and tax fees by 40% over a 2-year period. Accomplished results by developing technical skill sets of staff personnel and implementing the use of automated spreadsheets to provide efficient analytical tools and documentation.

- Successfully placed and completed multi-property securitized loan transactions approximating $70 million. Negotiated favorable terms for interest rates, release provisions and borrower operating covenants.

Professional History

Hamilton Partners Itasca, IL

Vice President - Finance (1990 - 2000)

An accomplished private equity group, acquiring, holding and managing a diverse portfolio of assets held by various affiliated corporations and partnerships. Reported to CEO.

- Upgraded financial reporting and analysis by creating a highly motivated team of five accounting professionals. Provided ongoing mentoring of team members to broaden and deepen their accounting and software skills.

- Achieved favorable tax efficiency in addressing a range of federal, foreign and state tax matters. Developed and implemented strategic tax planning approaches in concert with outside advisors.

- Initiated process improvements to treasury functions by fully integrating cash management for operating needs, short-term investment positions and maintaining appropriate levels for various credit facilities.

- Cost effectively directed and coordinated activities of various outside advisors in connection with complex acquisition and financing projects.

- Reduced interest expense on a foreign currency denominated loan by $800,000 over a 2-year period. Achieved by initiating and monitoring a fully hedged currency position.

Michael c. douglas: Michael_douglas@yahoo.com   Page Two

CHICAGO TRIBUNE COMPANIES   Chicago, IL
CONTROLLER (1988 - 1990)
Managed all financial reporting and accounting functions. Member of core management team addressing a broad range of key operating issues.
- Strengthened departmental budget variance control through more timely and frequent communication with operating managers forging a strong team approach to variance analysis.
- Substantially improved member satisfaction through more timely and accurate member billing. Accomplished by streamlining the monthly billing process and prioritizing key task dates.

PRIOR EXPERIENCE

CONTINENTAL BANK, CHICAGO, IL
CONTROLLER - MORTGAGE DIVISION

DELOITTE TOUCHE, CHICAGO, IL
SENIOR AUDITOR

Education and Professional development

Master of Science Degree: Accountancy – Brigham Young University, Provo, UT

Bachelor of Science Degree: Accountancy – Brigham Young University, Provo, UT

Certified Public Accountant – Illinois: Member of the Illinois CPA Society

Much has been said about the fact that some employers use a scanning method to review resumes. You must have your resume in a format to be readily scanned and easy to cut and paste for online submission. The Microsoft (MS) people have made that super easy for you. Save your resume in Plain Text. Here is how you do it:

Convert your resume to text so you will not need to "clean up" your text in the online application every time you copy and paste from your Word document.

- Open the MS Word document (*since almost all word processing is in MS Word, our directions refer to this format*) that contains your resume.
- Click File in the toolbar and select Save As.
- Type in a new name for this document in the File Name box.
- Under this is the Save As Type pull-down menu. Select "Plain Text"
- Click Save, close, re-open in Word.
- "Clean" your document only once by deleting extra page headings, deleting page breaks and fixing the spacing. You may want to put employment dates on a new line; Click Save.
- Close the document but stay in MS Word
- Reopen the document by going to File on toolbar, click Open, select file named "ResTextOnly.txt" and click Open.

Warning! If you are using MS Word, click on the icon for the file instead of opening in MS Word. If you open in MS Word, the document will become a Notepad doc...not what you want if you are preparing a resume for email. When you are posting online, simply open this document in MS Word; copy and paste to the online form.

KEY WORDS – Employers use key word to search resumes posted online or posted to a company database. These are skills, titles, expertise, and buzzwords represented as nouns and noun phrases. Examples: TQM, Vice President, CPA, SQL. It may be a good idea to add a key word summary to your resume that includes all potential job titles, skills and certifications and industry buzzwords. Look through posted ads for more word suggestions. However, your resume should be full of key words. Listing key words in a separate section may be distracting to the reader. You decide.

*****NOTE**: a key word section or section titled 'technical skills' is a must for IT candidates.

Following is an example of a resume with a key word section.

MICHAEL C. DOUGLAS
555 N. Hiawatha Avenue
Anywhere, IL 60000
(630) 555-1234
Michael_douglas@yahoo.com

> Use bullet points to indicate how you affected the bottom-line by 3 to 5 times your salary!

DIRECTOR OF OPERATIONS

Results-driven operations executive successful at building and leading goal-oriented teams; creating and implementing cross-functional processes; developed and nurtured strong working relationships. Sound business acumen with the ability to execute a wide range of operation strategies designed to establish customer relationships and increase revenue and profitability. A proven performer who moves easily from vision and strategy to implementation, follow through and completion. Demonstrated track record of making rapid assessments of diverse situational challenges and successfully developing and leading the resulting action plans.

Competencies

Strategic & Operational Planning	Strategic Alliances & Partnerships
Business Process & Strategy Development & Improvement	Major Account Development & Management
Quality & Productivity Improvement	Operations Management & Engineering
Customer Continuous Improvement Programs	Multi-Branch Operations Management
	System controls

Professional Experience

Insight Enterprises, Inc., Bloomingdale, IL (1996 – 2007)
Director of Operations

Built a seamless, cost effective operations team supporting an organization with $5 billion in annual sales. Partnered Operations with core business departments and developed high productive core-enterprise alliances. Member of select team of executives responsible for the tactical implementation of company initiatives.

- Saved loss of large client, over $1 million annually, by taking ownership of rollout schedules and continuously meeting with client to ensure expectations were met.
- Key player in merger of Insight and Brown Company; led teams in gathering client (both internal and external) requirements, developing processes and solidifying issue resolution to ensure a seamless transition into one ERP (SAP) system.
- Facilitated smooth integration of distribution center and production facilities into one warehouse after merger by ensuring needs for all business units were met and resolving any customer concerns.
- Implemented new processes and additional controls to reduce over 90-day balance by over 50%, from $10 million to less than $4.5 million increasing cash flow and allowing the company to regain compliance with bank covenant.
- Led teams as key player during SAP system conversion and upgrade. Provided requirement gathering, documentation, testing, and set-up, training documentation and training to assure seamless transition and eliminate impact to operations. Prevented several change requests that would negatively impact client specific needs.
- Negotiated past due payment issues with largest client that owed more than $25 million and established an escalation process to ensure ongoing prompt payments preventing the client from seeking a competitor. Received 90% of past due amount within 10 days.

Michael c. douglas: Michael_douglas@yahoo.com   Page Two

Insight Enterprises (cont'd)
Operations Manager

Successfully built, cultivated, and maintained long-term relationships, both internally and externally. Inspired trust with customers and employees alike. Implemented and monitored cost reduction measures while preserving customer service and employee satisfaction. Expanded the department role to address conflicts and issues that were both procedural and systemic across multiple departments within the organization. Identified root cause of critical issues (shipping delays, web issues, etc.) and establish processes and controls to prevent future occurrences.

- Scheduled and led weekly/monthly reviews with cross-functional departments; removed barriers across teams/areas to ensure cooperative efforts.
- Ensured customer satisfaction by continuously working with distribution center and configuration labs preventing and resolving issues.
- Developed and mentored several teams; set direction and established goals regarding: Field Marketing, Contracts Team, Minority Business, and Functional Business Analysts.

American Stores, Melrose Park, IL
Store Manager/Co-Manager

Responsible for all aspects of managing a store with $10.4 million in annual sales. This included budgeting, merchandising, inventory control, cost controls and customer relations. Developed and strengthened management and relationship skills.

- Created positive working environment that challenged individuals and rewarded those that accomplished the expected outcomes.
- Responsible for the planning and execution of major layout changes that were executed with minimum disruption to business.
- Motivated and directed large groups of people that were not direct reports but were integral players in completing required changes needed for new store startups.

Education

Bachelors of Science – Double major Finance & Economics, Elmhurst College, Elmhurst, IL
Associates Degree – Business Administration, College of DuPage, IL
Professional Development
SAP Courses
Management Seminars
Project Management

COVER LETTERS

As you whip up some terrific soup and get ready to serve it to a prospective employer, consider your serving presentation. Is it fine china or your everyday serving dishes? Your cover letter is simply a plate on which to serve your resume. When you apply for the job, design your cover letter for that specific job. Whatever style you choose, a good cover letter is a great introduction for your resume. Choose the right serving dish.

- **Keep your letter brief, easy to read**! If you are sending it through 'snail mail' always, use the same letterhead as your resume. Take as much care proofreading your cover letter as you do your resume.

- If you are emailing your resume, your cover letter should go in the body of the email. Add your resume as an attachment. Never send your cover letter as an attachment unless the prospective employer gives that direction.

- Target your letter to a specific person. Do not use "Dear Sir or Madam"; honestly, most women do not like to be addressed as madam, we don't. Take time to research who is receiving the letter. If you cannot find a name; for example, if you're applying from a blind ad, don't use a salutation.

- Once you have a name, use the person's formal title such as Mr., Ms. or Dr.

- Be detailed yet brief. State the name of the position and the person referring you in the very first paragraph. Include other details such as where you heard about the opening.

- Make a personal connection by addressing the individual by name or using a reference's name.

- Use bullet points to indicate how you are a good fit for the company. The bullets are not identical to your resume. They should indicate your "fit" using different words. Our samples use bullet points to highlight where you fit in the company.

- Remember; the point of sending a cover letter and resume is to get an interview. Use the cover letter to tell the reader you want a face-to-face conversation. Suggest when you will be calling them!

Following is a sample of how to write our favorite cover letter effectively.

MICHAEL DOUGLAS
555 N. Hiawatha Avenue
Anywhere, IL 60000
(630) 555-1234
Michael_douglas@yahoo.com

January 12, 2008

Aamco Industries
Attention: Nancy Burris
625 District Drive
Itasca, IL 60143

Dear Ms. Burris:

Joseph Hoolihan suggested that I submit my resume for your Sales Manager position. I believe that I am the candidate you seek for the following reasons:

- Surpassed annual sales growth by 18% for five consecutive years as sales manager.
- Increased new division sales 75% by implementing upgraded hiring and training program.
- Strong communication and writing skills; facilitated 25 national account presentations; proficient PowerPoint skills.
- Directed activities of 16 direct reports in six offices in five states.
- Averaged 13-15 days of travel per month working a five state area.

Currently, I am working on a development project for a manufacturing firm. I view this as a temporary assignment; therefore I have not included it on my resume. My main goal is to find a permanent position that allows me growth and opportunity.

In view of my experience and accomplishments, it would be mutually beneficial for us to explore how my services could be of value to you and Aamco. I will call you next week to discuss setting an interview appointment.

Sincerely,

Michael Douglas

ATTACHMENT

Letter that Directly Addresses the Qualifications Listed in a Job Posting or Ad

Your Name
Address
Phone & Email

Date

Full address of Recipient
Dear Ms/Mr. Recipient Last Name:

Discussion	**Statement**
Make the reference person's name the first thing in the opening sentence.	Jack Harms suggested I contact you regarding the Sales Manager position you're currently looking to fill.
Explain relevance of reference and why he suggested you get in touch. This is only appropriate if your contact actually knows specifics about the position.	He knows something of my past accomplishments and felt (*target company name*) might benefit were I to be on your team.
Transition line to show interest	I believe that I am the candidate you seek for the following reasons:
Assume what types of qualifications (e.g., years in the job, sales performance, communications skills, willing to travel, etc.) the target company would want in a candidate, and then provide a digest version of your resume concentrating on those things *Remember, the objective isn't to get the job. It's to get an interview.* *Include facts/numbers specifics to prove you capabilities. Avoid generalizations.*	Increased new division sales 150% by implementing upgraded hiring and training program.
	Averaged 13-15 days of travel per month working a five state area.
	Strong communication and writing skills; facilitated 25 national account presentations; proficient PowerPoint skills.
	Directed activities of 16 direct reports in six offices in five states.
Avoid discussing years you missed goals by averaging all years together	Surpassed annual sales growth by 18% for five consecutive years as sales manager.
"Ask for the order," which in this case is asking for that interview.	In view of my experience and accomplishments, it would be mutually beneficial for us to explore how my services could be of value to you and (*target company*).
<u>Do not</u> *ask them to call you. Be proactive... and make sure you call!*	I will call you next week to discuss setting an interview appointment.

Broadcast Letters

A Broadcast Letter is a "targeted" approach to job search. Your goal in sending this type of letter is to BROADCAST your capabilities to the individual that makes the strategic decisions at the company of interest. This person is the CEO or President, not the Human Resource Manager. In the Broadcast letter, you say how you develop a synergy with your skills and the company's goals.

To find appropriate target companies use the Internet and your local library for research. Many directories provide names of principals within the company. This can help you determine the name of the decision maker.

The Reference Librarian at your local library will be a great source of information. In addition, the following list of directories will help you find your target companies. We talk even more about resources in the Networking chapter that is coming up.

- Reference USA
- State Manufacturing and Services Directories
- Industry Directories
- Hoovers
- Thomas Register
- Sorkins Directory

Your resume should *not* accompany your broadcast letter. The Broadcast letter is communication to whet the appetite of the prospective employer. It should make him want to know more about how you can affect the bottom line.

MICHAEL C. DOUGLAS
555 N. Hiawatha Avenue Anywhere, IL 60000
(630) 555-1234
Michael_douglas@yahoo.com

May 31, 2009

Mr. John Van Overmeiren
VP Operations
Alumax Extrusions Inc.
1655 Powis Rd.
West Chicago, IL 60185-1668

Dear Mr. Van Overmeiren:

To remain competitive in today's markets, you are well aware of the never-ending need to find continuous improvements in the quality, productivity, cost and delivery of your products. Because of these needs, you may be in the market for someone such as me, who can design and implement the necessary systems to achieve these improvements.

I am a semi-retired senior executive seeking a part time position, or a short term project, with a small company such as yours, which can utilize my problem solving abilities and benefit from my diverse administrative and manufacturing management experiences.

As the former Vice President of Manufacturing for several small manufacturing companies, and Chief Project Manager for several consulting firms, I established an excellent track-record in bringing about major cost reductions and overall quality and efficiency improvements in their manufacturing functions.

If a highly motivated executive who is cost conscious, profit motivated, goal, quality and people oriented could benefit your company, I would welcome the opportunity to meet with you to discuss ways in which I can be of assistance in helping you achieve similar results.

Please contact me at your convenience if I can be of any assistance to you. Thank you for your time and consideration and I look forward to hearing from you.

Sincerely,

Michael C. Douglas

Thank you letters

Writing a Thank You letter after a job interview is a MUST. It is important that you view a Thank You letter as an integral part of a successful interview and not just a polite gesture.

If a major objective of an interview is to separate yourself from the other candidates, then you want to ensure that, just as with any other sales activity, you "close" the deal. Sending the Thank You note does that, it closes the deal of the whole interview process. Failing to send the Thank You letter allows other candidates to add that single bit of distinction that could sway a final hiring decision.

Writing a Thank You letter that includes small but important elements is important and reflects on the character and attention to detail you show in projects. This is another way to set you apart from other job seekers in a very good way.

One purpose of the Thank You letter is to reiterate what you believe went well in the interview. It is not the place to try to correct something that went wrong in the interview.

- A Thank You letter can also indicate your interest in the prospective employer and position, so it is appropriate to say something positive about the company and department where you interviewed

- Like any piece of writing, it is important to keep your audience in mind. If you're sending the Letter to a person who is likely of the Baby Boomer generation: i.e., his/her age is between 50 and 60 years, or to a traditionalist, send a handwritten note or one written on a computer; but send it through the US mail. It seems more personal, which is more in keeping with many Boomers' attitudes about business. Also write in blue ink. The perception is it is warmer and offers a more sincere approach.

- If your contact is younger than 50, a member of Generation X or Y, you can send them either a printed letter or an emailed message. An email is their traditional way of conducting business. Be sure to sign or attach a personal signature to this form, and again, use blue ink for the signature.

- Whatever way you choose to write the Thank You note, it is very important that you write one.

- Always include the time when you will follow-up after the interview.

Plan to send your Thank You letters within the first 24 hours following your interview.

MICHAEL DOUGLAS
555 N. Hiawatha Avenue
Anywhere, IL 60000
(630) 555-1234

Michael_douglas@yahoo.com

January 15, 2009

Mr. Jim Hart
Allied Gear & Machine Company
625 District Drive
Itasca, IL 60143

Dear Mr. Hart:

Thank you for taking time to talk with me about the Senior Sales Manager position. I appreciate your time and consideration.

As you told me, Allied seeks a person who is well versed in selling value over price and has solid time management skills. These are the very capabilities I have used in building successes with former employers. From what I learned of your organization's needs, I am sure I will be able to deliver the high level of performance you require.

This position is of great interest to me. In view of my experience and accomplishments, it would be mutually beneficial for us to explore in greater depth how I can be of value to you and Allied.

I will call you in the next day or two to determine the best time for us to meet again.

Sincerely,

Michael Douglas

Discussion	Statement
While a Thank You is more informal than an Introductory Letter, it's still a business activity, and unless the person specifically directed you to call them by his/her first name, use the last. A comma is OK as punctuation. Take the time to make sure you've got the person's name and it's spelling correct. Addressing a Thank You to Mr. Heart when the man's name is Hart won't help much. - During the interview, offer the interviewer your card and expect one of his/hers in return. Ask if they don't offer. - If you don't get one, ask the receptionist on the way out to clarify the spelling. - If no receptionist, check the company phone log. - If still no verification, call the company, explain to whomever answers that you need to send the interviewer a note, and you want to ensure you have the name spelled correctly	Dear Mr. Hart:
Open with a "thank you" for the interviewer's time. No need to say you know how busy they are…that's been said before.	Thank you for taking time to talk with me about the Senior Sales Manager position. I appreciate your time and consideration.
Review those elements of the interview that most apply to your capabilities.	As you told me, Allied seeks a person who is well versed in selling value over price and has solid time management skills.
Restate that you're the person for the job.	These are the very capabilities I have used in building successes with former employers. From what I learned of your organization's needs, I am sure I will be able to deliver the high level of performance you require

Discussion	Statement
"Ask for the order!" In this case, it is a second interview	This position is of great interest to me. In view of my experience and accomplishments, it would be mutually beneficial for us to explore in greater depth how I can be of value to you and Allied. I will call you in the next day or two to determine the best time for us to meet again.
	Sincerely,
	(Signed signature or email signature

Ready for the Soup? We like to think of it as liquid comfort. Here are some easy and delicious recipes.

Minestrone Soup

New England Clam-Chowder

Tomato Soup

Celestial Chicken Noodle Soup

Minestrone Soup

2 Tablespoons olive oil	1 cup chopped onions
2 cloves minced garlic	1 c chop carrots
2 quarts chicken broth	1 (15-oz) can kidney beans
1 (15-oz) can butter beans	2 cups shredded cabbage
1 (16-oz) can tomatoes cut up	
½ pound frozen cut green beans	1 cup chopped celery
1-tsp. ground sage	
1 tsp dried basil, crushed or ground	¼-tsp. pepper
½ pound frozen peas	

Optional: 4-6 ounces macaroni, Chopped fresh parsley, Parmesan cheese

Sauté' onions and garlic in olive oil until onions are clear. Add the rest of the ingredients except macaroni.

Bring to boil, reduce heat to very low, and cook for 1 hour.

In the meantime, boil water and add macaroni. Boil macaroni until softened but not cooked completely. Drain and wash with cold water, drain completely. Add to soup.

Continue cooking on very low heat for another hour. Serve with a garnish of parsley or Parmesan cheese.

New England Clam Chowder

2 teaspoons olive oil
½ cup diced celery
2 cups (1/2 inch) cubed peeled Yukon gold or baking potato (about ¾ pound)
1-cup water
1/8 teaspoon black pepper
1 bay leaf
1-Tablespoon all-purpose flour

1 cup diced onion

½ teaspoon dried thyme
1 (8-ounce) bottle clam juice
1 cup 2% reduced-fat milk
1 (6 1/2 ounce) can minced clams, do not drain
Chopped parsley (optional)

Heat olive oil in a large saucepan over medium heat. All onion and celery, and sauté 5 minutes or until onion is soft. Stir in potatoes and next 5 ingredients (potatoes through bay leaf).

Bring to boil; cover, reduce heat, simmer 12 minutes or until potato is tender.

Combine milk and flour in a small bowl, stirring with a whisk until smooth. Add flour mixture, clams to saucepan, and bring to simmer. Cook 2 minutes or until mixture begins to thicken, stirring frequently. Discard bay leaf. Ladle soup into bowls; garnish with chopped parsley, if desired. Yield: 4 servings (serving size 1 ¼ cup)

Tomato Soup

2-Tablespoons each unsalted butter and extra virgin olive oil
Two cups diced onions
1-Tablespoon finely minced garlic
½-teaspoon ground allspice
6 Tablespoons chopped fresh dill leaves
6 cups chicken or vegetable broth
2-cans (28 ounces) each peeled plum tomatoes, drained and chopped
1-teaspoon sugar

Melt the butter with the olive oil over low heat in a heavy pot. Add the onions and cook until soft, stirring occasionally, about 10 minutes.

Add the garlic and cook, stirring, for about 3 minutes. Sprinkle allspice over the onions; cook for another minute.

Add 4 tablespoons of the dill, season with salt and pepper, and cook for 5 minutes over low heat, stirring. Add the broth, tomatoes, and sugar.

Bring to a boil, reduce heat to medium-low, and simmer, partially covered, for 20 minutes. Remove from the heat and cool slightly.

Puree the soup in batches in a blender. Return it to the pot and stir in the remaining chopped dill. Serve hot or at room temperature.

Celestial Chicken Noodle Soup

12 cups chicken stock 2 cups cooked chicken cubed
Salt & Pepper ¼ cup butter
4 cups sliced carrots 1 cup heavy cream
4 cups cooked noodles Celery Salt

Combine 1 cup of stock and butter; bring to boil and boil rapidly until mixture is reduced to about ¼ cup (it should have a syrupy consistency). Stir in cream and set aside. Meanwhile, heat remaining stock to a boil. Add carrots and cook till tender. Add noodles and cook until tender. Blend small amount of flour (about 1 tablespoon) with small amount of cold water; stir to make a paste. Whisk into soup and cook until it thickens. Add cream mixture and chicken. Season with salt and pepper, and celery salt.

Makes 14 cups

Chapter 4

Networking...Don't Be Chicken

We like to think of networking as one of the main courses of a meal. But, most people chicken out! Networking is *powerful* and will feed your job search and sustain your career just as the main course of a meal will nourish and sustain your body.

Some of you might say that networking is fine for other people, but you are uncomfortable. You are not sure how to network or you think you don't do it well. You would rather eat bugs than look like a fool. You are not alone in this feeling. Many people really chicken out when it comes to picking up the phone, meeting new people, going to a new place alone, or talking about themselves.

What are you afraid of? Rejection? Is it too personal for you? Or is it just plain hard to do for you? Fear is a normal part of job search and if you are going to get a job, you have to face this fear and do it anyway.

> Don't be chicken…..
> As you begin your job search, network.
> As you continue your job search, network.
> If you have a job and are unhappy in it, network.
> If you have a job and love it, network.
> *Never* stop networking.

Our collective experience indicates that networking accounts for more new jobs than any other job search technique. It makes sense that this is something you need to do. Let's break this whole mysterious concept of networking into bite size pieces. Remember how to eat an elephant? Yep! One bite at a time. Learn to network; it can even be fun. Chickening out here is not an option.

Think of networking as a circuit board. On the board, all the wires cross in some fashion, but not all wires cross directly. If you give Joe a lead, he might not give you one back, but he might give one to Ann.

She then gives Jack a contact, who in turn might give you one. We are all in this together. When you give, you receive in some way. Be ready to support someone else. That person may not be the one who gives you your next lead. Just know that somewhere down the line you will benefit. It is another in the "pay it forward" concept. Networking is a marvelous marketing tool, with you as the product.

Career advisors have different ideas about what works and what doesn't with networking. Our philosophy is simple: Networking is an attitude and spirit that every individual should bring to life; it is not simply the thing to do to get a job or to get ahead in your career. If you think that networking is just for getting ahead or getting a job, chances are your impact will be short-lived, and that is not what we are looking for here. What we want is for you to learn to build a foundation that will last longer and produce sustained results in your work and life.

As we talk more about networking, we will tell you about some techniques that we know work. We will give you concrete tools that will make your networking more successful, not because of what you do, but how you do it.

Before we begin, here are a few facts to think about:

- A personal referral generates 80 percent more results than a cold call.
- Nearly 70 percent of all jobs are found through networking.
- Most people have at least 250 people in their networks, many have more.
- Six degrees of separation is true. (Anyone you want to meet is only five or six people away from you; closer in Internet social networking.)
- The purpose of networking is to give and get information. If you pursue networking properly, nobody feels pressured, used, or put on the spot. You are not selling yourself, you are telling about yourself. You are asking about others. You are exchanging information and building relationships. This is the true purpose of networking.
- The rest of this chapter serves as catalyst to help you build your network. Some of our suggestions may feel strange or different from the way you usually behave. If that is true for you, remember: you have given yourself permission to try some new things, to experiment with new ways of operating or behaving.

Give yourself a chance. Make a deal with yourself that you will try new behavior for thirty days at least. Thirty days allows a new behavior a fair chance of working and gives you a chance to integrate it into your everyday patterns. It could even become a habit. Just remember, it is a choice and that choice is yours.

Networking in job search is similar to networking in a new neighborhood. It is about people sharing information and building relationships. How did you find the best hardware store? Your dentist? The carpools? You went to a homeowner's association meeting, listened, and asked questions. You contributed when you could. You made friends and figured out the "go to" person on the block" and you went to him.

It is the same dynamic in a job search. Pretend this is not about you but all about information gathering. Pretty soon, you can stop pretending and realize it *is* about information gathering and relationship building. It really is as simple as that!

Remember; when you need a new relationship, it is too late to build it.

We believe networking is about an attitude, a giving attitude, and a few other things. Let's talk about the rules for a good networking attitude first. Then we'll discuss techniques to make the rules easy to follow.

Networking rule number one: Forget about who is winning. Networking is not a competition. Everybody wins the game if you play by the rules. Expecting nothing in return means giving, contributing, and supporting others without keeping score. When someone does something for you, you naturally want to return the favor. When you build a relationship, you are caring about people. Trust is evident. You trust them to do the best they can to reciprocate and help you the same way you helped them.

Networking rule number two: Don't be afraid, or do it anyway: Networking is not about having another person say the right thing or do what you want. It is about using the resources around you to further your goals by giving information and asking someone to help you. It's the asking for help that stops a lot of people. If you ask and the other person says no, you feel rejected. Look at it this way. If the other person can, they will; if not, there are other people to give information. Keep giving.

Networking rule number three: Ask for support. If you ask for what you want, you know what you need; it is a smart way to approach life. If you don't know what you want or need, nobody else does either. So know and ask. When you ask, you are clear about what you want. That includes asking for support. There is no pretense.

Networking rule number four: Beat the clock. Tackling a project alone takes way too much time and effort. By collaborating through networking, it is possible to do more in much less time. Collaboration builds relationships. Stop and think of ways to work with others. For example; help a colleague with research by investigating a new web site, or start a job club with some other job seekers. When somebody helps you, you help somebody else. Everybody benefits.

Networking rule number five: Be determined instead of aggressive. Networking is like planting a seed, nurturing it, and then watching it grow. Your focus here is to build strong relationships. In those relationships, there are people who want to help you meet your goals. As your relationships grow, there will be people who will help you before you ask. And, this is the most important part, be focused and do the same for others.

The definition of networking power is not how much you can get from others or how much they will do for you. Networking is powerful because the focus of the interaction and personal value generates collaboration in the relationship.

Networking rule number six: Look sharp all the time. Always dress for the job you want, not the job you have or don't have. If you want to be professional, look professional, act professional. This is a silent statement of who you are. Who do you want to be?

Networking rule number seven: Give more than you get. Self-explanatory.

Here's our recipe for making the networking rules work for you:

One of the most important ingredients is your self-introduction or Thirty-second summary.

A dazzling self-introduction is:

- Clear: Let people know what you do. You do not want any confusion here.
- Concise: Follow the KISS rule. (Keep it Simple Sweetie.)
- Distinctive: Be catchy enough to distinguish yourself from all the other people who might do what you do.
- Relatable: Use common words that create instant rapport.
- Engaging: Your words, mannerisms, tone of voice, and eye contact all contribute to attracting people to you.

According to a Harvard University study, the first seventeen words of your introduction carry the most impact. Do not waste words during that important time.

Here are some simple steps for creating your Thirty-second introduction:

Step One: Characteristics including a title: "I am a focused, detail-oriented financial professional"

Step Two: Experience: "I have over ten years of experience in financial reporting, analysis, operations, and negotiations."

Step Three: Education: "I have a Bachelor of Science Degree in finance from Duke University and an MBA from Keller School of Management."

Step Four: An achievement or unique statement about you: "In my last position I was extremely cost effective. I reduced supply costs 20 percent by developing and expanding the technical skill sets of staff personnel, streamlining processes and automating numerous accounting functions."

Step Five: Wrap it all together with what you can do for the company or organization: "With business foresight and the ability to communicate effectively with all levels of personnel, plus my innovative energetic style, I will be a valuable asset to any organization."

Now you have your thirty - second introduction'

"I am a focused, detail-oriented financial professional with over ten years of experience in financial reporting, analysis, operations, and negotiations. I have a Bachelor of Science Degree in finance from Duke University and an MBA from Keller School of Management. In my last position, I demonstrated a cost effective mindset by expanding the technical skills of staff personnel resulting in a reduction of supply costs by 20 percent. With business foresight and the ability to cut costs, I will be a valuable asset to any organization."

Our suggestion is to work with the tips and experiment. Present your introduction to friends who will be objective. Listen to what they say. Be original and inventive with it. Think of new ways to describe yourself. Your goal is to have a statement that is memorable, powerful, impactful, and true.

Now that you have something to say about yourself, delivery is your next step.

One of the most common fears we hear about networking is, "I never know what to say." We have partially solved that problem with your Thirty-second introduction. However, how do you initiate conversation in the first place?

It helps if you have something to offer—*and you do*. People will want to talk to you if they think you are a giver not just a taker. Talk about a job lead, job fair that is coming up, or a seminar you attended. We are talking about engaging others, drawing them to you.

Any comment or a question can provide an opening to attract others. Whether the comment results in conversation is not relevant. What is relevant is that you have graciously provided an opening to someone to connect with you. That is all we are after here.

Here are some conversation generators. Memorize a couple, and you will always have them along with your thirty-second introduction. If the opportunity arises, you will be ready.

- How did you get involved with this (organization, meeting, group, and event)?
- What a beautiful facility for a banquet!
- I hear the speaker today is an expert in (cooking, networking, wood working kickboxing).
- Can you tell me a little about this (organization, meeting, group, and event)?
- It looks as though we will have a full flight.
- This is my first time attending this (meeting, group, event, class).
- Is this your first time here? Let me introduce you to ------.
- I did not realize there would be such a crowd.
- Introduce the topic of eating: I wonder if they will be serving food? Almost everybody responds to it.

Two keys to being confident when meeting people are preparation and practice. Plan your conversation generators so you are comfortable approaching people. Practice with friends and in situations where you already feel comfortable.

Another problem people often share with us is they can't remember names. Most people can't. How many times have you heard somebody say: "Of course, I always remember names?"

Try this: **Focus, Association, Repetition, or F—A—R**

The **FAR** trick is a common method, but old as it is, it works. When you meet someone, get his name. If you don't hear it, ask to have it repeated: "I'm sorry, I didn't hear you. Your name is…?" Don't worry about offending the person. Who doesn't like to have someone ask who they are? Here is where it is important to have your introduction speech ready. You know what you are going to say. You don't have to try to think of something to say, so you can focus on the other person. Give them your complete attention.

When you get the name, associate it with something you talked about or something you will remember. Use their name in a natural way a couple of times in your conversation.

You are not alone if you feel awkward meeting new people or uncomfortable at new events. One way around this is to try to act as host, or volunteer at the sign-in table. You expect to greet people; it makes it easier, and when people sign in for the event, you can see their name and use that as an additional reference for remembering it.

And then, of course, there is the business card. This is another valuable tool for getting the word out about you. It gives people a tangible, physical way to remember you. We offer some effective ways to make the best use of this important little card in the next section.

But first, let's recap: We've given you networking attitude rules, some ideas about what to say, and we've talked about developing and growing relationships.

When you make a cake, you add the ingredients, you blend them together, and you bake it to get a dessert. Working with your network is the same way only you never stop baking. It is always in the oven, developing, growing, and changing. We call it nurturing your network. The word nurture means to promote growth and development. You can nurture your network so that it grows into a powerful entity of contacts and supportive relationships. Staying in touch keeps your network thriving.

Here are some easy ways to keep your network alive and well:

- Every week call one person you have not talked to in ninety days.
- Send a gift or note as soon as someone has done something for you.
- Invite people to join you in an event if you think it might interest them.
- Send clippings and articles from newspapers or magazines. When someone you know is in the paper, send them a copy of the article with a note of congratulations.

- Keep your note cards handy and designate some time in your schedule to write that note.
- When you think of someone whom you feel deserves a note, do it as soon as you can.

Have trouble writing a note? Here are some easy icebreakers. Remember, this doesn't have to be literary genius.

- Thank you for..........
- I appreciated............
- Your support yesterday..........
- I enjoyed reading about you......
- Congratulations on your recent......

The effect of a note is more than most people realize. The note reinforces the contribution, support, congratulations, or whatever you are acknowledging. A note brings the contribution alive for both parties. This is nurturing; it's developing a relationship and growing it for both of you.

Writing a thank you note or any note begs the question: Real mail or email? Email is faster, easier and an accepted method of communicating today. However, a hand-written note provides a personal touch that represents care, thoughtfulness, and sincerity. You decide. Whichever method is most comfortable for you, the important thing to remember is to do it. We talk about thank you notes in several sections in this book because they are important. They make you stand out as a person who is cares for others.

Some people have trouble receiving and accepting acknowledgment. If you are one who dismisses and tends to deflect acknowledgement, it's time to stop that now and think about this: It could be disrespectful. When someone gives you an opinion in the form of feedback, praise, or encouragement, accept the opinion graciously. What the person is saying is true for them. In addition, what they are saying might really be true for everybody, you just don't see it.

"Thank you" is always an appropriate response when someone acknowledges you or offers support. Develop your ability to receive and accept acknowledgement and support with graciousness and humility. You will discover a richness you never knew existed not only for yourself but also for those who compliment you.

Now you know the networking rules and you have your introduction speech. You know how to open a conversation and thank people for doing something for you. Next, know how to ask for what you want. A clear request makes it easier for people to respond in the best way they can. If you don't know what you want, we promise you, the people you ask will not know either. Be specific. Often that generates a trigger or prompts people to identify a contact or idea that will best support you.

Here are a few examples.

- Who do you know who…?
- Who do you know who I should know (given the following circumstances)…
- Who do you know who knows…?
- Who do you know who would benefit from…?
- Who would you recommend I contact…
- I would like to know who you recommend for…
- I am looking for… Who do you know…?
- I would like to know the names of people who know who…

Remember, people really like to be asked. Think about that fact when somebody in your network asks you for a contact or idea; aren't you pleased to know she thinks enough of you to ask for assistance? Asking is a way to empower, include, and recognize the people in your network for their resourcefulness.

And of course, if you do get a lead, be prompt with the follow up and the thank you.

Finally, trust and follow your intuition. Your intuition can assist you in responding to opportunities with power and clarity. When you learn to trust your heart, or inner voice, you will be more flexible, perceptive, and adaptable to situations around you. Allow your "heart" to help you and show you the way.

Now, let's talk about business cards. They can be one of the most effective ways for creating contacts for your network, finding new business, creating more business or most importantly, leaving a lasting and memorable impression for any of those three things.

Cards are not just for writing down recipes, not even our recipes!

Tips for business cards:

- Always have them with you.
- Get people to read them.
- Get people to keep them after they read them.
- Get people to read them, keep them, and remember you because of them.

First, make sure you have plenty. No matter what the event be prepared for a crowd. Carry them in a place where you can reach them easily so you don't have to fumble around to reach for one. Make it convenient to present one.

Some people immediately write where and when they met the person on each card they receive. That is a good habit but it is often awkward and distracting. We suggest doing your writing as soon as possible after the event. Just having someone's business card isn't very valuable if you don't have some network-critical information to go with it.

Next, exchange cards in a way that solidifies a contact. When you treat the business card you receive with respect, the recipient will also tend to treat your card and interaction the same way. When you are at a social occasion, your primary attention should be on the event. Be discreet when you hand out your cards. It will show.

Your business card is a great way to provide your contact information: name, phone, cell, fax, and email. We are now seeing LinkedIn information on business cards as well. It looks like this. (www.linkedin.com/in/yourfirstandlastname)

You decide how people can contact you. Your card should be professional looking. Too much information could give a cluttered appearance.

When you give out your card, do not discuss:

- Any four letter words or any word you can't use on the radio
- Anything relating to sexual innuendo
- Issues relating to sex or gender preferences
- Religious conviction
- Political views
- Ethnic background
- Opinions on multi level marketing programs (pyramid selling)
- Anything controversial about current events

And do not:

- Engage in self praise
- Mock someone else.

We all have personal experience relating to each of these "never never say" phrases, which is why they are in this book. They are our experiences. They happened. Learn from them.

Whenever you get a business card, look at it. Say something positive. Later, you might jot a name or something about the person on the card.

If the meeting is less than memorable and it happens, consider what you tell your kids: Remember the Bambi movie, when Thumper's mother looks at Thumper and says, "If you can't say something nice, don't say anything at all." Maybe you can't say anything that wouldn't sound phony, so smile, and be kind. That also goes a long way. A caring attitude shows in many ways.

Handing out your business card is like a game. If the person you give it to keeps it, uses it, maybe even passes it to others, you win. If he doesn't pass it along or remember you; well, you lose. So, use the "Three W" rule: Some Will. Some Won't. So What? But, of course, you want to win. So the more remarkable the experience you have, the better the chance of winning the business card game.

Here are some ideas for making your card more memorable.

- Write in longhand on the front of the card, "See the back." Then write in long hand on the back, the name of a web site, a quote, or maybe a personal note from you. Make up something on your own. The intention here is to get the person to remember you with your card serving as the reminder.
- Buy a box of star stickers. Put a gold star beside your name on your card. Or use another kind of sticker. We have seen smiley faces. You decide.
- Add a title after your name. We have seen, John Jones, Grand Poobah, Designated Hitter, and Top Dog. Our personal favorite is Rich Sanders, G.S.D. We had no idea what those initials stood for, so we asked. It started a conversation, which is exactly what the card was designed to do. This incident happened five years ago and we still remember it and wanted to share it. Oh, the initials? They stand for Gets Stuff Done. What would you remember about the guy who gave you that card?

Fill the back of your card with some pertinent information. We have seen cards with:

- A short recipe; preferably one from this book
- A current year calendar
- Phone numbers for major airlines
- Las Vegas odds on various games
- A local sport's team home schedule
- Your resume points (another quick way to advertise)

Some other techniques:
- Use a different shaped card.
- Print your information in portrait format instead of landscape.
- What about a photo? If you decide on a photo, get it professionally done.
- Use a hologram.
- Hand out a magnet or a bookmarker.
- If you have an unusual name, put the phonetic spelling next to it, for example: Sally Coek (Coe).
- If you do business internationally or if you are bilingual, put your name on the back of the card in the language, you speak or in the language spoken where you are doing business.

These are just a few ideas. Be creative. Creativity is memorable.

What should never be on a card? Avoid:
- Creases or bent edges, staples, stains or dog ears
- Typos
- Aging, fading, or discolorations. If cards no longer look good, get them redone.
- Your name written in
- Cross outs and corrections. Get new cards.
- Anything off color. It is simply in bad taste and very memorable for the wrong reason.

A business card is a great networking tool. Don't leave home without them.

Another great tool is what career people call a "handbill." According to the dictionary a handbill is: A commercial solicitation designed to sell some commodity, service.

For example:
Companies try to sell their products using advertisements in the form of placards, television spots, and print publications.

It is also: A public notice.

For example: Jack placed an advertisement in the local newspaper to inform its residents of the upcoming garage sale.

Those definitions can also apply to career development and networking. The handbill acts as an advertisement for you. It is a public notice telling people who you are, what you do, and how they can help you--all on one sheet of paper. A handbill is indispensible in formal networking meetings when everyone is there to spread the word about him or herself. The handbill, with your thirty-second introduction, is the key to advertising you and telling people what you want.

Create your handbill

Your handbill is a snapshot of your resume; but it is shorter and more concise.

Handbills are usually one sheet of paper offering:

- Your name and contact information
- Your profile summary
- The position you are seeking
- Your key accomplishments
- Your industry expertise
- Your employment history
- Your education
- Your target companies or where you want to work
- Your professional affiliations

Most handbills contain this information for obvious reasons. However, in addition to your contact information, the category that to us is the most important is *target companies*. This is the information that tells everyone who reads your handbill where you would like to work. You are asking them who they might know who knows somebody who works for that company; in other words, you are asking for a contact or connection into that company.

Recently we facilitated a networking group in which one networker listed his target companies and the man sitting next to him said his neighbor is the CEO for that company. The two exchanged phone numbers and the networker had his resume hand delivered to the CEO when the executive was outside watering his lawn. This is the goal of every networker: To get their resume hand delivered with a good word about them to a person of influence in their target company. It doesn't get much better than that.

Remember one of the networking rules? Ask for what you want. When you are in a networking group, read off your list of target companies and ask if anyone knows someone at one of the companies. Indicate that you would love to talk to them. That is a clear statement saying: "This is what I want and this is how you can help me."

It is important to remember here; if you don't know what you want or where you want to work, the group doesn't know either. And if they don't know, they can't help you. It is imperative to focus your search. Focusing your search means do your homework and line up your target companies. One networker told us he changes his targets every week. That's fine, but when he speaks from his handbill, he speaks in specifics and his group knows what he wants on that day. More about target companies later in this chapter.

The format of your handbill is as variable as a menu. Here are a few ideas:

- Give yourself a colorful logo and use it on the handbill.
- Format it with distinction with boxes or shading.
- Use brightly colored paper.
- Leave a space for notes. Whoever reads your handbill might want to jot down a few things about you.
- This document is a take home to everybody, make it memorable.

When you create your handbill, take the time to do it well. Your handbill is about you and, like your business card; you never know where it could end up. It should advertise you in the best way possible. Proof read it.

Target companies

Target companies are places you would like to work. They are companies you have researched and meet your criteria for your preferred:

- Industry
- Company size
- Values
- Location
- Career growth opportunities
- Culture

Those characteristics are just starting points. There may be much more criteria you want in your next place of employment. Our suggestion here is to go back to the assessment chapter. What did you write that you hated about your jobs? What did you love? This is the information you should be looking for when you research what you want in a target company.

We suggest you chose ten companies as your targets for your next job. Ten is a workable number to use at networking events, memorable but not over-whelming.

You can discover a whole bunch of information just by searching the Internet. It is a valuable resource. If you do not know how to use the Internet or a computer, learn now.

Community colleges, public libraries, and even some job clubs offer computer training, often free of charge. There is not a job in the world today that does not use a computer or the Internet in some way. Now is the time to learn how the computer can help you change your life.

Things you can learn about a target company:

- If the company is not for profit or for profit
- The company's management and how it works
- Who the officers are
- Their SWOT (strengths, weaknesses, opportunities and threats)
- The company's financial situation
- Number of employees
- Who serves on the Board of Directors
- Location(s) of headquarters, branches and subsidiaries
- And anything else you want to spend the time looking for

Information is power, and with the Internet you become Superman or Wonder Woman.

Where else can you get information? Public libraries have a host of resources. Ask for a business librarian. Most public libraries have them, and they are always willing to help you.

Hoovers, a business information directory, is a great source for information available at most business libraries. The online version requires a paid subscription to access.

Try: www.SIC.com for a reference point to get started with your research. Another online resource is www.manta.com, and it is free with registration.

Of course, you can always search for a company by name. That is the easiest, most obvious way, but it does not always give the most complete information. Researching target markets is just that; research. It takes time and patience. Both pay off when you decide on a place where you want to work, and because you know a lot about the company, you are comfortable and happy with your choice.

Cold Calling isn't just for take-out food

We have yet to meet anybody who likes cold calling. So, here is yet another place where you are not alone. However much you dislike it, cold calling can be an effective way to get your foot in the door in a company. Just like every other technique we have discussed, it works. To be a good job seeker, you have to try everything and keep trying everything until something clicks and you are on your way to your next job. (We keep repeating important things.)

The phone is a powerful tool when looking for a job. It requires no travel and allows you to contact a lot of people in a short amount of time. We are going to share some useful ways to use the phone wisely and well.

Remember, most people find it hard to make cold calls. But your lack of enthusiasm must not be evident when you make your calls. They require an upbeat attitude. You can hear negativity, whether you know the person, you call or not. So work on getting upbeat before making your first cold call. And, remember, the more calls you make the more confident you will become, and the *easier* (no kidding) it will get.

So don't stare at the phone, get moving. If you were making one of our main dishes, you would start by getting out the ingredients and the cooking equipment. What are the main ingredients of a job seeking phone call?

Start with a phone script. Write out what you want to say exactly as you want to say it. This exercise will help you present yourself effectively; you won't be fumbling around for the right words.

Your script should contain five parts:

- Your name
- Your job objective: Begin with: "I am looking for a position as_____." Often if you say you are looking for a job, you will be interrupted or stopped. Avoid the word job.
- A statement about your strengths or what you could contribute to the company. This can be almost the same as in your 30-second introduction. Spend time editing this section. You want it to sound natural; you will have to do a lot of rehearsing to make it sound like it wasn't rehearsed.
- A good worker statement: "I am reliable, hard working and a quick study."
- A goal statement. What is your goal? It might be an informational interview, a networking connection, or a job interview. If it's an interview say: "When may I come in for an interview?" (Remember to ask for what you want; this is another way to do it.)

Keep your script short. We think a good statement should take about thirty seconds, much like your thirty-second introduction.

Write your script the way you talk. Make it sound natural, the way you usually speak.

Now for the rehearsing. Do it a lot, in front of a mirror, standing up and smiling. It makes a difference. You do not have to memorize it. You can keep your script in front of you when you are making the call.

Who do you call now that I have a script? We suggest calling people you know first. We call this warm calling. It is your warm up, getting comfortable making calls. It's like pre-heating the oven to make sure you have the right temperature when you put in the cake.

It is not always easy speaking to a hiring authority; but again, persistence will pay off. When you call your target company, ask to speak to the manager of the department where you want to work. This might be tricky because many companies use automated caller menus. If you get a menu, pressing zero or just hanging on usually gets you to an operator or a human who can direct your call.

Don't ask to talk to the human resources department unless that is where you want to work.

When you get the manager's name, write it down right away. Make sure you have the spelling and pronunciation right. Make sure you have the job title correct. Then you can use it in your conversation. You may need it later to send a thank you note or a resume.

If you do get to speak to a person, do not ask about a job. You might be told there are no openings, be directed to human resources, or be told to send your resume because there is no one you can talk to about a job. You do not want this result.

When you get to speak to a person, tell them you want to send the manager some information and you want to use the correct name and title. Get that information, thank the provider, and hang up.

Then call back the next day with the name and title, and ask to speak to that person.

Often in large companies, the receptionist screens callers just like you. This might be a way around that problem, call when the receptionist is out to lunch or just before working hours or just after. At those times, the person covering for the regular receptionist may not have the screening experience and may put you through. It happens.

What about voice mail? If you get voice mail, you are closer to having a cool call rather than a cold call. We do not recommend leaving messages on voice mail. You can check the pronunciation of the name, and that is good. Here again, try calling first thing in the morning. If you don't get your party, keep trying. At least you have a name, title, and pronunciation. This is progress.

If you have a referral to the person you are calling, mention that as soon as you reach your target person. For example: "Falice Platt suggested I call you." This opening will at least give you a polite audience for the short time you want to keep this person on the phone.

Sometimes, in addition to the receptionist, there is a secretary screening calls. If the secretary asks what the call is regarding, say a friend of the person you are calling suggested you speak to her about a personal matter. This is a true statement and a good way to get to talk to your target person. Congratulate yourself for having gotten around yet another obstacle.

Now think about the goal of your cold calls. If it is an interview, ask for an interview. You might be told there are no positions open now. You can say, "I would like to come in and talk to you about the possibility of future openings."

If they tell you the company is not going to be hiring for another six months, switch to requesting an informational interview: "I would like to learn more about what you do and how the industry is evolving. I know you are a leader in the business. I would like to learn more about how you manage the market." We're talking persistence here. This scenario can be uncomfortable and maybe more assertive than you usually are; this is why we suggest practicing these statements with another person or to yourself, over and over until you can say it smoothly.

Sometimes asking for an interview doesn't make sense. If you get that hunch, ask for other industry contacts. For example, "Do you know anybody who might have this information?"

If the person you called sounds rushed, ask to call back at a specific time and date, then do it. Or ask if it would be okay to call back every week or so to check whether the person has any new information or leads. Take the initiative to call.

Following up with your contacts may be one of the most effective processes of your entire job search. It is also the key to cold calling. You would be surprised how many people will remember you said you would call back and you didn't. And don't forget your thank you notes.

They are like putting salt on a tomato. You can eat it without the salt, but it tastes a lot better with it.

That wasn't so bad, was it? Remember the "3 W" rule, some Will, some Won't, so What? Rejected? That's good. You have learned. The next time will be easier. Theodor Seuss Geisel also called Dr. Seuss had his first book rejected by 29 different publishers before Green Eggs and Ham went to press. Don't give up.

If you get the interview, be sure to send your resume before you have your interview conversation. Congratulations! Have a big piece of chocolate cake. You've earned it.

If you landed an informational interview, don't send your resume but bring several copies with you to the meeting and have a piece of chocolate cake. (You could gain weight just making phone calls.)

Another cold call tip; set a goal to make a certain number of cold calls a day. As coaches, we usually assign ten a day. More is better, and we encourage doing it at specific time each day. Make cold calling a habit.

After all is said and done, what it the absolute worst thing that can happen because of making these cold calls? Think about it.

Prepare yourself for the meal

When you sit down to a meal, the food is always more appealing if it is presented well. You can have the best thirty-second introduction, a great handbill and a beautiful business card. You know everything you want to know about the companies where you want to work, but if you do not look and sound professional, you will lose all you have gained.

Think about your image and your behavior. What is your presence? What is the atmosphere you create? At one networking group, the participants were all sitting around a conference table taking turns with their thirty-second introductions. When it was one young man's turn, he stood up straight and spoke his introduction. Standing up transformed him. He carved out his space and claimed it assertively. He was memorable. He had presence.

Think about that when you walk into a room. You create your presence. If you slouch when you walk into a room, you may be turning people away without even knowing it. So stand up straight put your chin out; looking any other way shows less confidence.

Dress appropriately. Business casual is the usual dress for networking meetings. That means for men, cotton pants and an open necked shirt.

For women, a dress, slacks or a more casual pants suit with flat shoes. Remember, networking groups often have employers attending. You never know who may see you. Consider your grooming and wardrobe when you go. Save the shorts and jeans for picnics.

Another image enhancer is your handshake. We recommend a firm and open hand, no limp fingers. Women tend to extend their fingers, which creates a weaker handshake. Some men have told us they tend to shake hands lighter with a woman who has this type of handshake.

If you are a woman reading this, don't you want equality in the work place? Demonstrate this by returning a handshake with a firm, confident grip. A firm confident grasp of another's hand in agreement or greeting, levels the playing field, no matter what the gender.

Here are the elements of a firm handshake:

- Extend your full hand, don't cup it.
- Hold the other person's hand firmly; no squeezing, this is not a strength contest.
- Shake hands palm to palm, with your thumbs interlocking.
- Shake hands three times maximum.
- Make eye contact, smile.
- Be confident, it will show.

When you meet someone and make eye contact, it shows you are paying attention. Show interest in what the other person is saying by listening and looking the person in the eye. Eye contact should begin as soon as you engage another person in conversation. Be sure to make eye contact when you say good-bye; it will leave a pleasant lasting impression.

We have had people ask us, "Where do you keep looking to maintain eye contact?" It sometimes is unnerving and can be viewed as intimidating when you look someone directly in the eye for a sustained time.

Here is one technique that works: Try looking first directly in the other person's eyes. Then begin looking at a place just below their nose, the place between the lips and the nose. Look there for much of the time as you are talking. It is not quite direct eye contact, so it is less aggressive but this method shows attention and interest in the other person.

If you glance away, return your gaze quickly. Avoid looking over the other person's shoulder, as if you are looking for another more interesting conversation. This looks as if you are bored and ready to move on. Clearly, it is not the impression you want to leave.

If somebody is looking you up and down, chances are they have more than business on their minds.

Where are the networking places? Actually, there are many good options.

Job clubs are networking groups. Each has its own flavor or personality depending on its founders and facilitators. Shop around for the group that works for you.

Support groups can be small or large and are a very helpful part of the job search process. There are specific types of support groups for the unemployed. Spouse support groups are available as well. Don't under estimate the value of individual, marital, or family groups. You can also get support and someone to talk to who has been through the same thing.

Industry job clubs such as manufacturing, information technology, or food groups keep you updated in your particular industry. Don't forget professional associations or alumni groups in your world of influence.

How do you find a group for you? Start with churches, libraries, and state employment centers.

Churches are traditionally your first line of defense against going the job search alone. If you belong to a faith community, you have a support system in place already. Make an appointment with the pastor, minister, or rabbi. He has a pulse on the resources in the area. In addition, often people in the faith community will offer to be of help in their particular companies with job leads and industry contacts.

There are a number of churches or faith organizations that offer help to people of all religions. Jewish Vocational Services offers a variety of programs for all people. The Church of Latter Day Saints offers a great job search workshop. Take advantage of the generous usually free offerings.

Libraries are another excellent source of help during the job search.

Reference or business librarians are underutilized. Their job is to help. Just ask!

If they don't have the answer, librarians will find it for you. Often libraries set aside a designated area for the job search. Are you making the library part of your search?

Libraries also collaborate with service organizations and can be meeting places for job clubs.

Libraries are always looking for funding for their community services outreach programs. If a job club meets at a library and gives the library their attendance sheet, the library can use it as resource for state or federal grants. In return, the job club gets free library meeting space.

It's a win-win situation.

If your library does not have a job club, start your own job group there. Then you will have a legitimate purpose and title: job club leader. You can use that title when calling employers for job leads to share with your club. That call can also lead to other exchanges of information. We call this a cool rather than cold call. It might be easier to ask for information or positions if it is for your job club and not for yourself. It works. Cool.

State sponsored and funded employment organizations are cropping up across the country. Most states adopt the "one stop shop" approach: Within one building you can collect unemployment, sign up for the job skills matching service, take classes, check job openings, and use work stations. Sometimes job clubs or industry groups meet at state facilities. Look in the phone book or go online to search townships or counties that offer employment services.

Accountability groups and boards of directors. It is vital in the job search to build accountability into your job search process. Others held you accountable at work. Now you need people to help you hold yourself accountable in your search.

Having your significant other be your accountability buddy is asking for trouble. While that person cares for you and has a stake in your successful job search, He or she is too close to offer an objective point of view. Keep your significant other in the loop, but step outside the home for job search accountability.

Accountability groups are sometimes run at employment centers, but often job seekers start their own accountability groups. Here's how it works. You pick five people you respect, trust, and share common interests with. The interest could be geographic location, industry background or simply that you like them for their positive energy. Set a time each week to meet, and set some ground rules.

- No disbanding the group until everyone gets a job.
- No one puts another down.
- Each individual's goals for a meeting are set by that individual.
- Progress on goals is reported at the next meeting.

- Time is set aside for discussion or suggestions.
- The person who does not meet goals buys coffee for all.

See how being accountable works? We know of a group of five individuals that continued to meet once a month even after each of them got jobs. Now they are working, they all have the same goal to continue to network. Their group keeps them focused on that goal.

Board of directors is a creative way to keep you focused and informed about your field or industry. For your board, choose employed people whom you admire and respect. This is not a group of cheerleaders. They may not always agree with you, but that can prove valuable if what you are doing in the search is not working. You will select a board of directors to advise, encourage, and offer another objective, professional point of view that could turn your search in another, more successful direction.

Here are a few ways to build a board for yourself.

- Meet once a month, maybe a Saturday morning or early evening. Remember people have jobs and are giving up their time.
- Be respectful of their time. Consider and research their suggestions carefully, even if you disagree.
- Send thank you notes.
- Volunteer in their causes. Offer to give back in some way. (Networking Rule Number One again, what can I do for you?) When your board meets, the way you give back is to listen and act on suggestions.
- Group dynamics tends to be more powerful; this is why group meetings work best for everyone.

Research indicates that 72 to 75 percent of folks get their jobs through networking. This leaves 25 to 28 percent of your time to devote to other areas of search.

Here are a few other tips that are creative, often overlooked and rarely used. What this means is, you'll encounter less competition:

- One gentleman opened up the telephone book and started calling companies of interest. He hit pay dirt on the third call! Before you do this, you need to have a thirty-second summary. See Chapter 4 for ideas.
- Cold calls intimidate most people in a job search but are very effective for just that reason. Few people do it!

- Get dressed up, resume and cards in hand, and start knocking on doors. Try an office park or industry park to maximize your time. If a place will not accept resumes, at least you can get a business card and follow up with a phone call or email. This works well if you are in sales or facilities management. It shows your initiative and that you are not afraid to make those calls.
- Bring flowers to the receptionist of one of your target companies. This actually got a job candidate an interview, no kidding.

Now that we have talked you into networking, try some of these great dinners. This is the only kind of 'chickening out' that is acceptable in your job search!

Teri's Chicken Marsala

Rosemary Chicken

Clancy's Favorite Chicken

Hot Chicken Salad

Chicken Marsala

½ cup dry Marsala wine
½ teaspoon dried tarragon
¼ cup Italian-seasoned breadcrumbs
1/8 teaspoon garlic powder
2 teaspoons olive oil

1-teaspoon cornstarch
1/8 teaspoon salt
2 Tablespoons grated Parmesan cheese
4 (6 ounce) skinless, boneless chicken breast halves
2 cups hot cooked angel hair (about 4 ounces uncooked)

Combine first 4 ingredients in a 1-cup glass measure, stirring with a whisk until blended

Combine breadcrumbs, cheese, and garlic powder in a shallow dish; stir well with a whisk. Dredge chicken in breadcrumbs mixture. Heat oil in a large nonstick skillet over medium-high heat. Add chicken, cook 4 minutes on each side or until done.

Microwave wine mixture at high for 30 seconds or until slightly thick, stirring once. Arrange chicken over pasta, top with sauce.

*Some people add sliced, sautéed mushrooms to the wine sauce.

Yield: 4 servings (serving size 1 chicken breast half) ½-cup pasta and about 2 tablespoons sauce.

Chicken Rosemary

2 ½ lbs of chicken pieces
1 minced garlic clove
½ cup olive oil
½ tsp. rosemary

Fine dry bread crumbs (seasoned)
Wash and dry chicken pieces and put in a shallow baking dish. Sprinkle with salt & pepper. Add remaining ingredients except breadcrumbs. Then sprinkle with bread crumbs. Marinate for several hours, turning now and then and adding more crumbs.

To cook, put on rack on broiler pan about 6" from heat. Brown for about 25 minutes on one side and about 15 minutes on the other side until golden brown.

Clancy's Favorite Chicken

2 tbsp. All-purpose flour-(doubled 4 tbsp.)
¼ tsp salt-(1/2 tsp)
¼ tsp ground black pepper – (1/2 tsp ground black pepper)
2 (4 oz) skinned, boned chicken breast halves (4)
2 tsp Olive oil-(4 tsp Olive Oil)
½ cup chicken broth-(1 cup chicken broth)
½ cup dry white cooking wine or any white wine-(1 cup dry white wine)
1 tsp or more Parmesan cheese-(2tsp or more Parmesan cheese)

Preheat oven to 350°
Combine first 4 ingredients in a flat pan or pie dish.
Dredge chicken in flour
Heat oil in an oven proof skillet over medium heat
Add chicken, cook about 2 minutes on each side, chicken should be lightly browned
Add broth and wine to chicken
Bring whole mixture to boil, remove from heat
Cover and bake at 350°for about 30 minutes or until chicken is done
Sprinkle with parmesan when you are ready to serve

Hot Chicken Salad

2 cups diced chicken
½ teaspoon salt
1/8 teaspoon ground pepper
1 Tablespoon grated onion
1 ½ cup minced celery
1 cup low fat mayonnaise
2 Tablespoons lemon juice
½ cup slivered almonds
½ cup buttered croutons
½ cup grated sharp cheddar cheese

Mix all ingredients together except cheese and croutons and turn into greased baking dish. Combine croutons and cheese, spread on top. Bake 15 minutes in at 450°

Chapter 5

Interviews...

The Main Course

Preparing for an interview is similar to making a new recipe. If you are hungry, you can savor the new dish even before preparing it. The same is true for a job. You want the job so bad you can almost taste it. Preparation is the key to a landing a job. Preparation is the most important ingredient for a successful job interview and a successful job search.

So before you go to the interview appointment, prepare everything you need to be ready to serve yourself to the prospective employer. In this chapter, we'll tell you how.

Too many job seekers picture the interview process as an athletic competition. They assume the challenge is to score points for content and style with each question; i.e., the better the answer the higher the score. If they do really well with the interview, they win the job offer.

This is not exactly the way it works. It is true you, this is an evaluation and you are justified in wanting to appear articulate, credible, and professional. But you also want to accomplish the five goals of acing an interview. Here they are.

1. Build rapport
2. Create a relationship that will last beyond the first interview
3. Understand and address the potential employer's concerns and priorities
4. Treat the interviewer like a friend, not an adversary
5. Emphasize your ability to fit into the organization

Your strategy with every interview should be to paint a consistent picture of yourself that develops and reinforces fundamental themes.

As you know, there are many ways to answer a question and some are a lot better than others. Of the good answers, your challenge is to utilize the one that will be the most effective given your circumstances.

The trick to a good answer to an interview question is to know the intent of the question. The key to delivering a confident answer is...what? Yet again, preparation. We're not saying you need a memorized, canned response delivered right on cue, but rather give serious thought about how to respond to certain issues that may come up during the interview BEFORE the interview.

Your preparation for any interview should focus on two concepts:

- The employer's needs, priorities, and values.
- How your skills, abilities, aptitudes, values, motivation and personal style will benefit the employer, so the interviewer gains an accurate picture of your worth for this job.

Now let's talk about how these two concepts synergize so your interview produces the best snapshot of you.

Here's the good news: There are really only three interview questions. No kidding.

Regardless they are ask, the employer really wants to know:

- What value can you add to the enterprise as an employee?
- Can you prove it?
- Why do you want this job?

There is risk on the part of the company when a new employee joins the organizational mix. In the interview, it is your job to eliminate this risk by describing the value you will bring to the company.

The prospective employer seeks to minimize risk through the rigors of an interview. As such, every interview question probes some dimension of your capability or motivation. You are selling solutions to the needs and priorities of the company.

Your solutions are:

- Your expertise in the form of knowledge and technical skills
- Your experience or transferable skills
- Your motivation: the roles and responsibilities that fire you up

Though it may be difficult during an interview, you need to think when a question is asked: What's the point of this question and why is he asking it?

A good illustration is the standard question: "Where do you see yourself in five years?" You, no doubt, have a ready answer but stop just for a minute, view this question as an opportunity to demonstrate the serious thought you've given to your values, priorities, and driving motivational forces.

Your response should reflect optimism. You should be doing a reality check on where you do want to be in the next five years. Does this company offer what I think is best for my future career goals? Think over your answer ahead of time. In addition, re-think it again before actually giving it voice. Consider why is the prospective employer asking the question and then dovetail your answer to what the prospective employer really wants to know.

So, what does the employer really want to know? Who knows where anybody will be in five years? But, this is a place where you can show the employer that you have plans, and those plans can fit well into what the company is cooking up for the future.

Example: *"Of course, I don't know precisely where I'll be in five years. No one can know that. But I certainly want to be in a position where my management and technology skills will give me a career edge."*

If you're asked an inarticulate or imprecise question, use your answer to provide useful information, validate what you sense are the interviewer's underlying concerns, and then reality test your response by asking, "Have I addressed your question fully?"

Even though the interviewer's question was not clear, you were; and you didn't make the interviewer appear wrong in the process. Challenging the interviewer's interviewing skills would not be a good way to achieve your goal of building rapport or landing the job.

Avoid patronizing, pontificating, or professing. You gain little by trying to out-think or out-maneuver the interviewer. You probably lose a lot more. You gain more by communicating a desire to be responsive and sensitive to the interviewer's needs. Personalize the interaction and build the relationship by being positive and collaborative. Ask if you have answered their question. Ask if the interviewer needs any more information?

It is common to struggle with interviewing even though you have all the necessary skill and abilities to do the job. Keep in mind the invitation to an interview indicates the hiring manager believes you may be the right candidate. The interview is to determine whether you are qualified and if you are likely to fit into the company culture. It is important that you use the interview to determine whether you could be successful in the position and with your potential boss, staff and peers. The interview is for both you and your potential employer, which is why we call it a collaborative conversation.

Interviewers often use shortcuts to eliminate candidates. One method is to rule out potential employees based on a first impression. Based on the first seven to ten seconds of what the interviewer subjectively sees and feels about the candidate before asking any questions. Just like the aroma of a dish usually tells you whether you're going to like it or not, an interviewer can decide during these critical first seconds whether he thinks you're right for the job. Preparing carefully ahead of time will help you get past this first impression screening. When you walk onto the company grounds, every person you see, or don't see, can potentially hurt or help your job quest. Keep that in mind.

When you enter the reception area, generally somebody from the company will come and get you at the door. Make eye contact, give them a firm handshake, be prepared for small talk, and work a compliment into the conversation and smile, smile, smile. In the networking chapter, we gave you lots of information to make this greeting easy and comfortable for both of you.

A few of the things you can do to ensure successful first impressions are:

- Prepare your clothing a day in advance. Try on your interview clothes and ask for suggestions from professionals you trust. Whatever the prospective employer's dress code, you should dress at least one-step better for the first interview.
- Research the company and the community so you are familiar with the area.
- Know how to get to the interview location and where to park. Leave sufficient time to arrive at least ten minutes ahead of your interview. It is a good idea to make a "dry run" by going to the interview site a day or so before your scheduled appearance. *(Do a trial run at the same interview time so you can check out the traffic and travel times.)*
- Be polite and respectful to everyone you meet.
- Sit up straight and look alert while waiting for the interviewer.
- Show enthusiasm about the company. Research the company so you can mention relevant aspects in your first statements. Show interest in the job.

- Bring several resumes. Carry them in a nice looking portfolio.

The elephant in the room

When you know someone wants to talk to you about something but is not doing it, be the one to bring it up. Get it out in the open. "When there's an elephant in the room, introduce it."

In this case, the elephant might be your age. Many people worry about how age will affect their chances of getting a job. We had a client who sported a wonderful mane of white hair. This man sent a broadcast letter to a company president and got an interview. Keep in mind; he got the interview without anyone seeing his resume or him.

When he walked into the office, there was a pregnant silence from the company's thirty to forty year old executive staff. The president of the company was about forty-five and the oldest employee there. Without missing a beat, the candidate put out his hand and with a great deal of energy said, "Looks like you need some grey hair around here." That broke the ice, and the client could then present how his experience would profit the company big time. He did get the offer, along with two others, but chose another company. So much for the excuse, "I'm too old."

Be comfortable being who you are and what you have to offer. There is an upside to everything. The up side is what you must present.

Your interview can be your signature dish

Many career coaches, including us, suggest you choose three words you would like the interviewer to use to describe you after the meeting. Then make those words drive the interview.

For example, if you choose compassionate, energetic, and trustworthy as your three words, use them throughout the interview, in your stories.

"I get energized when I do team building presentations for clients."

"In my annual reviews, former employers would always highlight the fact that I was compassionate."

Find adjectives that are genuine and you will be able to work them into the conversation.

During an interview or while networking, remember to use the name of the person you are speaking to often. The sound of their name is like music to a person's ears. Think of it as the spice in a recipe, subtle but necessary for the final dish to taste just right. Try using a family member's name more often when you talk to them and see how comfortable it feels. It makes the listener feel your focus is on him or her alone. The gesture creates a nice feeling. That's what you want the interviewer to be feeling about you.

First impressions and body language

Here's a second helping of first impression information. How long do you have to make a first impression? Seven to ten seconds, that's it! A negative first impression may be impossible to overcome no matter how great you are and how solid your credentials. So what makes a first impression? Basically, it is body language. What does your body language say about you? Are you portraying yourself as confident and appropriately enthusiastic? Do you appear arrogant and pompous? Maybe you are shy, but you don't want the shyness to be mistaken for lack of interest or self-importance.

We communicate with words but a great deal of our communication is visual. Look at some of the world's best-known business leaders. They have a commanding presence; they ooze confidence and charisma. You can and must do the same thing during a job interview. Strong and effective body language is an important part of an interview conversation.

With a little work, you can improve your body language and increase your chances of an invitation back for another interview and eventually for getting a job offer. When you are interviewing, you may be so nervous you are not exhibiting what you really feel. You don't want to show that you are nervous, so your body language may be stiff. You may have trouble getting the appropriate words out of your mouth. Maybe you don't know what to do with your hands and when you sit down you find yourself jiggling your legs, twisting rings on your fingers or other distracting behaviors.

Let's review some things to be aware of when you walk in the room for that all-important interview. Have you ever observed two men shaking hands when both want to dominate the situation? If you are not involved, it can be pretty funny, or sad depending on your viewpoint. Picture two men coming towards each other with hands outstretched to shake. Suddenly, one grabs the hand of the other and quickly tries to turn the hand over so his is on top! But the other man doesn't want to give in so he keeps holding fast. Before they know it, a little arm-wrestling has begun.

What does all this mean? Power! The one with the hand on top has perceived power over the other. This is aggressive behavior and, we promise, it won't work well in a job interview. When you get that handshake in an interview, you can pick up a little hint about the interviewer. What's the hint? Sounds a little silly but the next time you see a powerful businessperson shake hands, watch and you see.

We do not recommend the power handshake. Prepare yourself for a good handshake; make sure your hands are dry and as you introduce yourself, wait for the interviewer to initiate the handshake. Respond with a firm, quick shake. Shake and let go. You don't need to hang on. We talk more about the handshake in networking tips.

As you are going through the handshake, remember to have a warm, friendly smile on your face. Make and keep eye contact, say your name clearly, and make certain you say the interviewer's name. If you don't catch the name, there is nothing wrong with asking the person to repeat it. Names are important to people and we live in a global environment so you are going to hear names that are not familiar. Ask for clarification so you pronounce the name correctly.

Wait for the interviewer to invite you to sit down after introductions. If you are seating at a conference table, it is appropriate to set your portfolio on the table. However, if you are seating across the desk from someone, remember that the desk is the personal space of the interviewer. Do not set anything on it.

There is no specific encyclopedia of body language though you will hear many opinions about what a specific action means. Pay attention to your posture, where you put your feet, and make eye contact with the interviewer.

Here is how some basic body language might appear to others:

- Arms folded across your chest suggest a defensive, closed posture. You may also appear uninterested and disconnected from the conversation.
- Jiggling legs, wiggling a foot suggests nervousness. Instead, plant your feet on the floor or cross your ankles. Being nervous is natural during a job interview, anchoring yourself may help you be still.
- Avoiding eye contact or staring at the floor or off into space suggests shyness that may look like lack of interest.

- Slouching in the chair indicates a lack of discipline and maybe even lack of preparation for the interview.
- Touching your face shows discomfort and that you might not be answering questions honestly.

Some of these actions have reasonable explanations. You may slouch simply because you have poor posture, but these actions may be misconstrued. Even if you don't have perfect posture, sit up straight and mirror the interviewer. Don't make the mistake of *mimicking* the interviewer; smile back, nod your head at the right moments and maintain eye contact. (Eye contact is important. Review our networking tip about it.) You want the interviewer to be doing the same thing you are doing – sitting relaxed or leaning forward.

If you notice the interviewer looking at his watch, fidgeting or leaning back in his seat staring in another direction, you might be losing his attention. If that is the case, regain his interest by asking a question or throwing out an achievement statement.

As the questions continue, answer and speak directly to whoever asked the question. If more than one person asks questions, be sure to glance at each person quickly, but always go back to the person speaking or asking the question.

A good way to improve your body language is to see and hear yourself as others see and hear you. Practice interviewing in front of a video camera. Ask a friend to be the interviewer and stage the camera to catch your whole interview from the time you enter the room to open the interview until the final handshake. We always recommend videotaping practice interviews to our clients.

Make sure you use all the tools we will discuss in this interviewing chapter: your thirty-second summary, your "reason for leaving" statement, your answer to questions about your weakness, and your achievement statements. Critique yourself honestly; ask a friend to review the video with you and look for instances where you can improve.

Even if you fall off the chair during the interview or the interviewer dozes off during your achievement statements, finish the interview with confidence. Thank the interviewer for his time; ask what the next steps are and when you might call back. No matter what happens, every interview teaches you something. When it's over, ask yourself what you did great and what you could have done better. Then determine what you can do to improve.

Now that you are ready for the challenge of interviewing, let's discuss some issues that may arise.

Employment Gaps

First up are employment gaps. Many people feel that any time off between jobs translates into a huge negative for employers. Not necessarily! It depends on how you dish it up. Are you defensive? Do you feel guilty? Do you get the "deer in the headlights" look when asked the question, "Why have you been out of work so long?"

What is the appropriate answer? First consider: Is there an acceptable amount of time to be out of work? The answer is no! To you, any time out of work is too much, but you can't be sure how the potential employer feels. Second, ask yourself: What is the interviewer really trying to learn by asking questions about gaps? Actually, the interviewer wants to know what you've been doing with your time. So, make it easy on them– say what you have been doing!

If you have been working part-time or are in a survival job you may not want to add that to your resume, but you can mention the situation in your interview.

For example:

> *"Actually I am currently working on a development project for a manufacturing firm I view this as a temporary assignment; therefore I have not included it on my resume. My main goal is to find a permanent position that offers me growth and opportunity."*

Note: Regardless of what this example shows, we recommend that if you have been involved in a consulting or contracting position in your field of expertise put it on your resume and application.

Let's consider how you fill in the gap when you have been looking for a job for a year or so and have not taken a temporary job. What do you think the prospective employer really wants to know? More than likely the real question is, "What have you been doing all this time?"

Sprinkle a little flavor into your interview by sharing what you did to make the world a better place. Add some of your volunteer work and community service to your resume. If you are using the functional or combination format, it is easy to add a bullet point regarding how you are affecting your community. Your work in the community can tie in very effectively with your job title and industry experience. Even if it doesn't, adding that morsel of information gives the employer a taste of your personal values and community commitment.

Often when you are searching for a job, you can make time to take a class, add a certification or foreign language to your list of accomplishments. Maybe you did research pertinent areas of growth in your industry. Explore what funding is available through your local government to cover the cost of training. Adding Six Sigma training or a Project Management certification will add a colorful garnish to your main dish.

Perhaps you were fortunate to have a good severance package and you took the opportunity to travel. Or maybe a family situation needed attention, such as an aging parent, family illness, or young children. The prospective employer is concerned about how your personal situation may affect your commitment to your new job. So, allay the fears.

For example:

> *"I was able to take advantage of the time to travel. It was a wonderful opportunity! Now, I am ready to return to work and I am very interested in your organization. This position is a good fit for me because...."*

Or:

> *"My father became very ill and needed constant care. That situation has resolved and I am now completely prepared to return to work. My skills are a good fit for your organization because....."*

Another example:

> *"My children needed me at home. That is no longer an issue as they are both in school. I also have a back-up plan for school holidays and illnesses. My family is very supportive of my returning to work."*

Remember, time spent away from gainful employment can be a positive. Look for ways to weave the experience into your interview.

Donna, a stay-at-home Mom did just that in her resume and subsequent interviews. Donna was out of the paid workforce for over 25 years. What was she doing all that time? Well, she was raising a family, serving in her church and in the community. Donna was the volunteer director of a genealogy center and principal of a religious education program. As a volunteer, she had numerous other unpaid experiences. She managed other volunteers, maintained a budget, did fundraising, and positively affected the lives of children, teenagers, and adults. Donnas' prospective employers valued her volunteer experience and today she is happy and working.

If you have employment gaps, prepare yourself to answer the questions that might make you uncomfortable. As with cooking, preparation and adding a unique spice or flavoring is imperative to interviewing success.

Illegal questions

Certain subjects are taboo at a dinner party. Discussing religion or politics is just asking for trouble. The same holds true in interviews. There are illegal questions. Federal and state laws prohibit employers from asking about:

- Race
- Gender
- Religion
- National origin
- Sexual preferences
- Birthplace
- Age
- Disability/marital/family status

Employers generally avoid these topics. Discussing these topics in an interview and then not hiring the candidate? Well, there may be grounds for a discrimination suit *(though it is very hard to prove)*. However, we all know that some people do not follow the rules. Human Resource professionals are usually aware of what is legal and illegal. But, others involved in the hiring process may not be as up-to-date on the legislation.

If you are asked a question that appears illegal to you, always go to the intent of the question before deciding whether to answer it or not. For example, if your interviewer asks whether you are a United States citizen, you could reply I have authorization to work in the United States.

Alternatively, if your interviewer asks if you are married, you can reply with these questions: How does this is question relate to the job? Or why do you ask? You can try to change the topic or respectfully refuse to answer. Or you can answer the question, illegal or not. We would wonder about the intent with that question.

Federal and state laws prohibit prospective employers from asking certain questions that are not job related. Questions should be job-related and not used to find out personal information. People have ways of finding out what they want to know. You have to decide if you want to tell people the information, report them, or not answer the question at all.

A prospective employer is trying to eliminate risk when hiring a new employee. If you have young children, if you are heavily involved in your religion or if you have a moral viewpoint contrary to most individuals in a company, the prospective employer may consider you a risk. Is this fair? Probably not, but it is a reality.

Many women have suffered through the question: "Do you have children?"

You could answer with the standard question: "How does this question pertain to my job?" That is usually a safe answer if you say it with curiosity and not sarcasm or contention.

Or, for example, the interviewer says there is some overtime expected and if you have children, could this be a problem for you, you could reply, "That has never been a problem for me before." If the question of religion comes up, you could simply say, "I consider myself a spiritual person and live with a sense of respect for all people." In other words, answer the question in a way that limits the topic and gets the message across that you are not going to go into any depth on these subjects.

Another example, if you are asked about your age, try humor, "I am definitely over 21!"

There is always the option of filing a charge of discrimination with the United States Equal Employment Opportunity Commission. This is usually not productive. You have to prove the discrimination is deliberate, and that is very difficult.

If you already worked at the company, you might have more of a case. However, during a job interview, the interviewer could plead ignorance and probably get away with it. And where does a claim get you in the job search? Certainly not the job. Spend your time on a positive, proactive approach, it's just smarter.

Keep in mind you can always answer the question. It may turn out to be to your advantage. A minority-owned company may want to hire other minorities. Women with children understand other women with children. Single parents understand other single parents.

The prospective employer is taking a huge risk by hiring you. Keep that in the forefront of your mind. Do what you can to eliminate the risks.

And remember that once you are hired, an employer may legally request the following:

- A copy of your birth certificate
- Affirmative action statistics
- Your marital status (married or single only)
- Proof of citizenship
- Photograph for identification card
- Physical examination and drug testing
- Social Security card

Be prepared for all the questions thrown in your direction. Attitude goes a long way in achieving success.

Reason for leaving

Many people feel defensive when having to explain why they left their previous employer, even though the stigma of losing a job passed about 15 years ago. "Why did you leave your last position?" seems to give many job seekers that deer in the headlights look. The best way to avoid looking like a serving of "road kill" is to have your answer prepared. Let's call this your "reason for leaving" statement. Preparing a statement in advance will prevent you from blabbing on and on and giving the interviewer all kinds of information they do not need to have.

Do not ramble. Instead, organize your statement around only four points:

- What prompted the action
- Your impact on the position you had
- Your contribution to the company
- Your next positive step

Example:

1. As in many organizations these days, my former company was undergoing some changes. *(This is what prompted the action)*.
2. The company had to redistribute headcount the restructuring affected me. *(The impact on your position was to eliminate it)*.
3. However, while I was there, I reduced overhead expenses more than ten percent annually by developing and implementing a

centralized approach to inventory. *(One of your contributions to the former company)*.

4. I am interested in using my skills in management and logistics in a company like yours. *(A positive next step that will affect the new company.)*

The bottom line is you need to be very comfortable with your answer. Once you have designed your answer, practice it over and over until it becomes conversational. You have to be at ease with what you are saying. Practice in front of a mirror or with a friend. Be certain to make eye contact with the interviewer. Eye contact shows your credibility about what you are saying in an uncomfortable situation.

Do not use negatively charged words such as fired or terminated. There are positive words to describe a negative situation, use them instead.

Following are words to use that convey the information in a positive way. Use these words to fill out applications too.

Words to explain your Reason for leaving

- Career advancement
- Temporary
- Economy slowed
- Business closed
- Family needed me (no longer a problem)

- Career change
- Relocation
- Downsizing
- Job ended
- Rightsizing

- Seasonal
- Reduction in Force
- Restructuring
- Educational/ skill upgrade
- Health or injury (no longer a problem)

Remember not to talk negatively about a current or past employer. Generally, this type of conversation reflects poorly on the job seeker rather than the past employer. Negativity makes you appear not be a team player or to be difficult to get along with. You never come out on top when you are describing your former boss, company, or position in off-putting language. Stay positive! Use this opportunity to mention that your former company provided you with great experience and that you learned a lot that you will bring to a new opportunity.

Keep in mind that whether you are moving to a new position through choice or circumstances, you want to present yourself as taking a step up and making the best move for your career. Your purpose here is to persuade the prospective employer why you will be a benefit to his organization. The interviewer has to understand why hiring you will be the best thing for his company and his bottom line. No matter what has happened in the past.

State Your Accomplishments

Now we are getting to the meat of the interview: accomplishment statements.

The best way to make a lasting, positive impression is to use a statement that allows you to emphasize your worth to an organization. Your accomplishment statement can answer these questions:

- What is one of your strengths?
- If we called your last employer, what would he say about you?
- What can you do for this company? Why should I hire you?
- I have interviewed people with more experience than you, why should I hire you?

To write an effective accomplishment statement, start by identifying specific successful achievements. Review the assessment chapter for some ideas.

For example:

> *"A few years ago my previous company faced some significant financial challenges. I initiated a centralized approach to inventory. In addition, I opened national accounts for office space, furniture, equipment, and vehicles."*

What powerful words describe this accomplishment?

Cost effective
Resourceful
Focused
Detail-oriented
Productive
Forward thinking

This exercise helps you remember some of the great things you did at your former company and reminds you of valuable contributions you made. Take the powerful words that describe your achievement and write a statement using "I am." Take a moment and repeat the statement aloud.

I am… cost effective…
I am …resourceful…
I am…focused…
I am…detail-oriented…
I am…productive…
I am…forward thinking…

Do this in front of a mirror and really listen to yourself. Feels good, doesn't it? Reward yourself for your good work by reviewing one of the main dish recipes and decide what you are going to make for dinner, or you could have more of Sally's Hot Chocolate.

Now, let's put the actual statement together.

1. I am *(powerful word)*
2. Give an *exam*ple of a problem you had to work through and what action you took to solve the issue. (Hint – look at your achievement.)
3. Indicate the result.

Here we go:

"I am cost-effective. For example, at my last company I reduced overhead expenses more than ten percent annually by developing and implementing a centralized approach to inventory. In addition, I opened national accounts for office space, furniture, equipment, and vehicles. This allowed us to take advantage of key pricing strategies that are successful today."

Using a commanding statement to answer an interview question leaves the employer with some definite evidence that you will do for his or her company what you have done in the past.

An accomplishment statement can also be useful to get an interview back on track. For example, if you had to explain an employment gap or an uncomfortable departure from a former company, once you have made your explanation, end it with a power statement, leaving a positive result in the mind of the interviewer.

Remember to construct your "reason for leaving" statement. Follow that statement with a power statement such as this one:

"While I was at XYZ Company, I initiated a new marketing campaign for their latest product. As a result of this campaign, sales increased 20 percent within the first three months."

Your Weakness Statement

For some reason, interviewers believe it necessary to ask about your weaknesses. It's almost like being on a witness stand in a courtroom. We are not advocating lying or even stretching the truth, but you do not have to give information that is not required.

"What is your biggest weakness?" is a question that could make you look bad. Don't let it happen. Prepare yourself because this question comes up repeatedly. We think it isn't about your weaknesses but about how you answer an awkward question. Let's review some ways to answer this question to make you look great!

Consider turning a weakness into strength, but make it real. Don't try the old, "I'm a workaholic or I'm a perfectionist." A prospective employer does not want to hear those old, overcooked statements. By using these answers, you are essentially telling the employer that you are not going to answer the question. This is not the best strategy in a job interview.

If you want to turn a weakness into strength, use a weakness that you identify and correct.

"I felt my skills in process control needed some polishing. My former company needed to improve process control so I became a Six Sigma Black belt and increased customer service response 10 percent within six weeks."

The last thing you want to do is share a major weakness that will prevent you from getting the job such as:

"I really have anger issues and I do not like working with a team."

Forget about it, that will put an end to the interview will end very quickly, and you'll be without the job. What you need to do here is show that you have the ability to realize a potential weakness and find a way to overcome it. Here is one that many people deal with:

"Public speaking has been an issue for me so I signed up for Toastmasters and learned how to address a group in a professional way. Now, I find that I am good at speaking to large and small groups on a variety of topics."

You can also admit something minor that doesn't affect your job.

"I am really a neat freak; at the end of each day I make certain that the top of my desk is absolutely clear."

Honestly, who doesn't like someone who is neat? This answer isn't as good as the others mentioned, but it might help you move the interviewer onto another topic.

The last thing to try is humor. And, really, it does not work for everyone. If the interviewer is not in a good mood, if your timing is bad, the statement will fall flat leaving you with more than egg on your face.

One of our clients tried answering the weakness question by saying (with a very serious face) that kryptonite was his only weakness. Hmmm. The interviewer had experienced a long, hard day and this was the last candidate she interviewed. Guess what? She didn't have a clue as to what he was talking about. The candidate had to explain that he was like Superman. Well, it wasn't too funny. Save that one for your kids

Possible questions to ask an interviewer

There are times during an interview when you know you have answered the question correctly and the interviewer just sits there and stares at you. What do you do then? Frequently, job seekers start rambling. Before you cook your own goose by giving unnecessary information, consider this.

A better way to handle an intimidating interviewer or maybe an interviewer who doesn't know how to interview is to sit quietly and wait for the next question or peel off a few questions of your own. If either of these situations happens to you, you can save the interview and possibly still get the job by having some questions to ask in your apron pocket

Here are a few possibilities for questions that could save the day. Have a couple of these questions memorized. Remember this is your interview to save if you have to. Prepare, Prepare, Prepare.

1. How would you describe the responsibilities for this position?
2. How would you describe a typical day in this job?
3. What is the company's strategy for moving forward?
4. What kind of training would I receive from this company?

5. When does the training program begin?
6. What are your expectations for this position?
7. What do you see to be the major tasks and challenges of this position?
8. How would you describe this organization's management style?
9. What are the prospects for growth and advancement?
10. What are the strategic issues facing this company?
11. When do you think you will be making a decision about this position?
12. How much travel is normally expected?
13. Is this a newly created or established position?
14. If this is not a new position, what did the previous employee go on to do?
15. Is there a clear career path within your company?
16. What changes do you foresee in your organization in the next few years?
17. What makes your organization different from similar organizations or competitors?
18. What is your organization's biggest challenge?
19. Does this position require a lot of individual work, group collaboration or both?
20. How frequently do you relocate company employees?
21. Is there a relocation policy within your company?
22. Is it possible to be transferred from one division to another?

More Tidbits...

Just like everything else in the present day job search, interviews are changing. First, you will have more of them; and second, they are no longer just face-to-face with the hiring manager. You may have a group interview. Sometimes the interviewers will be your potential peers or your subordinates. (No kidding, this is happening more and more. Subordinates may actually pick their boss.)

If you applied online, an email screening is your first obstacle. If your resume is selected via the email screen, next, it will go to the human resources resume reviewer. This professional will look over your resume for experience and other information they believe the most qualified person will need. If you are still a candidate, you may be screened by phone. You may undergo all of this before you ever talk to a human resources professional inside the company, who will do yet more screening.

There is keen competition for every job, so you have to be smarter with your job search plan. Notice that strategy! We say smarter with your job search plan.

Here are the facts. When you apply for a job, it is usually in a field where you have some experience, education, or background. If you don't, often the company's screening policy will eliminate you early. Of course, there are exceptions and we'll talk about them later.

So, you have applied for a job, and you have the required experience and education. These two factors alone should get you past the initial screening procedures. But remember, minimum qualifications got your competition through, too.

In your resume, you have provided your contact information, both email and phone. Most job seekers use their cell phone as their primary contact tool. If the cell phone is your choice, what does your recorded answer say? If you are using a home phone, make sure you have a professional sounding message.

Please do not have a recording of a child, music, mention of pets or children in your answering message. If you do share a phone line, think about getting a number for which you alone are responsible. If your answer recording is yours alone, you will not miss a call; you can check voice mail as often as you want, and your voice mail is password protected so nobody can get to it but you.

Now what do you say? Keep it simple. Here are several good professional messages:

- You have reached Jack Harms, please leave a message with a call back number; I will return your call as soon as I can.
- You have reached 630-555-4567, please leave a message with a call back number, your call will be returned as soon as possible.

If you must share a phone, work out how you will get messages and what your voice mail message will say before you get a call from a prospective employer. Leave nothing to chance.

We have found if you don't work at everything that detracts from your image as a serious professional candidate; a prospective employer will find your vulnerability every single time. So skip that stressor and anticipate.

Let's say, you have sent a resume and you have been pre-screened and you are still in the running. Be prepared for a phone interview by having a phone interview log. Then when the call comes, you will have that company's information at your fingertips. Your phone log should include:

- Date you applied for this job and how (networked in, on-line, other)
- Company name
- Job description
- Qualities you have that match that job description
- Name and title of a contact person with this company, if you have one

We suggest keeping a copy of the resume you sent for a particular job clearly labeled with the company name and what job you applied for with that resume.

When a prospective employer does call (and they will), you do not want to say: "Now what job is this about?" You want them to think this company is the most important company you want to work for. Any other impression is unacceptable.

If you are returning a message, provide your first and last name and the job you are calling about. If you are unable to return a call during business hours, return the call as soon as you get the message. If the prospective employer called at 1:30 p.m. and you didn't get the message until 5:30, call back then. Voice mail is your friend here.

Remember, the prospective employer may be working late, so be prepared to interview then. Just like the Boy Scout, always be prepared and always anticipate so there are no surprises.

Here is your decision. If you are quick with your responses and feel confident about what you know about the position, you may want to talk then.

If you feel the need to compose yourself first, ask for the time. Make an appointment to talk to the person when you have all your paperwork in front of you. This should not be a detriment to your chances unless this is a position where fast thinking and extemporaneous speech is a real plus, and they are testing you.

You can always say something like: "I'm really glad you called, but I am just on my way out the door. I can give you only five minutes now but I would rather call you back when I can give you plenty of time and my full attention." Make an appointment to do just that. *Always offer to call them back, and get their phone number.* Try to take the initiative. Then you'll at least know your chances of talking to that person again are pretty good. It is not a certainty but you are taking control, which is demonstrated leadership; and you can prepare yourself completely for the call.

You deserve a nice 'meaty' recipe after all of this hard work. Here are some favorites enjoyed by our significant others.

Steve's Favorite Pot Roast

Stuffed Pork Tenderloin

Oven Beef Stew

Pop Morrison's Meat Loaf

Steve's Favorite Pot Roast

3 lb Chuck Roast
10 3/4 oz. can cream of mushroom soup (mixed with ½ can water)
1 package onion soup mix
1 lb. baby carrots
3 or 4 potatoes cut in chunks
1 large onion cut in chunks

Mix water and soup together. Place roast on foil and sprinkle dry soup mixture over roast. Spread mushroom soup over top. Wrap securely with foil. Bake at 325° for 2 ½ hours. Add vegetables and cook for another hour.

Stuffed Pork Tenderloin

Prepare your favorite stuffing recipe.
Halve two pork tenderloins of equal size split open lengthwise (do not cut through) flatten.
 Season with salt and pepper.

Spread the stuffing over one side of the tenderloin; lay the other side over the top. Season with salt, pepper, and top with 4 bacon slices.
In order to hold the stuffing in place, you may need to tie the tenderloins together with string.
Place on rack in open roasting pan. Roast in a slow oven (325°) for 1 ½ hours. Makes 8 servings.

Oven Beef Stew

2 lbs beef stew meat   1 large onion quartered
1 lb baby carrots   4 stalks celery (chopped)
½ green peppers (chopped)   2 c sliced mushrooms
1 large can chopped tomatoes   ¾ c dry red wine
¼ c tapioca pudding   ¼ c breadcrumbs
1 tsp. salt & ½ tsp. pepper

Brown meat to seal flavors. Combine all ingredients in a large Dutch oven. Cover with a tight lid. Bake in oven 4 hours at 300°. DO NOT UNCOVER WHILE COOKING.
Delicious served over pasta.

Pop Morrison's Meat Loaf

1 lb ground beef
1 c Italian bread crumbs
1 beaten egg
½ lb ground pork
¼ c minced onion
1 Tbsp. minced garlic
1 tsp. salt
¼ tsp pepper
2 Tbsps mustard
1 Tbsp ketchup
1 Tbsp BBQ sauce
1 Tbsp Worcestershire sauce

Mix all ingredients thoroughly. Spread in ungreased large loaf pan. Bake in 350° oven for 1 ½ hours. Allow to set for 15 minutes before slicing. Be sure to save some for sandwiches.

...Prepare to be 'Grilled'

An interview often feels like a grilling. Sometimes the heat is turned up too high. So to prevent you from getting burned, let's review the types of interviews you will encounter.

As the job market gets more and more competitive, employers are becoming more inventive in their methods for finding exactly the right candidate. We have identified nine types of interviews.

1. Screening interviews

This is generally the initial interview with a recruiter from human resources. Usually this is the first time you are invited into the company or enterprise. The purpose is to see if you meet preliminary requirements. You want a return invitation so your objective should be to sell yourself. Avoid discussions of salary and benefits. Guard against the temptation to evaluate the job before it is offered. Be prepared to use your thirty-second summary and your accomplishment statements to prove to the interviewer you are the best choice to move forward to the next round of interviews. This may also be the time for you to complete an application.

For applications, we suggest bringing a cheat sheet. Have all your information with you to complete this document. Even though it is your life, people forget things. Again, hear our favorite mantra: Prepare, prepare, prepare.

2. Phone interviews

Many companies use a phone interview as a substitute for a face-to-face screening. You may be asked to do either or both. Your phone interview may or may not be with a hiring person, but it is always with someone who can give you thumbs up or down. Here are some tips and techniques that will give you a competitive edge.

- Keep your phone charged.
- Have paper and pen with you.
- Have your phone log in front of you.
- Have your resume in front of you (*You would be surprised how easy it is to forget something that is on your resume and it is very likely the prospective employer probably has it in front of him.*)

- Be sure to write down the name or names and position or role of the person or people interviewing you. You may want to refer to that list later.
- Ask if the interviewer can hear you. If you can't hear the interviewer, say: "I am having trouble hearing you." Don't struggle and possibly miss an important comment.
- As with any interview, be prepared to ask some questions at the end of the interview.
- Don't chew gum, drink, or eat.
- Have a plan for a quiet room where you can talk without interruption or background noise.

This will sound strange, but you sound better standing up than sitting down. And smile when you talk; it makes a difference in your voice. One of our clients took phone interviews in the bathroom. It is quiet and you can lock the door. He stood up and faced the mirror so he knew he was always smiling.

You might want to practice interviewing on the phone with a friend or accountability buddy. Get comfortable talking and answering questions on the phone. Use an earpiece or Blue Tooth; if that is what you are familiar with; if you aren't, this is not the time to try new equipment.

Just as with a face-to face-interview, don't feel you have to fill the silences, but be prepared with appropriate questions if the opportunity presents itself. After the call, as with any interview, write a thank you note.

Few people are hired solely on a phone interview, but it is one way to test the waters for both you and the prospective employer and to narrow the field from semi-finalists to finalists. Be as professional on the phone as you would in person. Try to relax and be yourself. Few people can put on an act in the bathroom.

3. Behavioral interviews

Behavior-based interviews have been around awhile and are now the interviewing standard. A behavioral interview does not mean prospective employers watch to see if you touch your nose or crack your knuckles. They are not judging your behavior during the interview. The premise is your past performance is the best predictor of future success. What you have done in the past is an excellent predictor of what you will do in the future.

Employers want to hear specific examples that illustrate key skills and experiences. You will know you are having a behavioral interview if many of the questions begin with: "Tell me about a time when...," or "Describe a situation where...."

This is different from an interview in which you are asked for opinions or ideas. Here is where you can highlight your achievements rather than what you hope to accomplish in the future.

Once again, the main ingredients are preparation and research. Think about what you've done or experienced what most closely relates to your potential employer's key issues: either problems you have discovered during your research or an issue you anticipate happening going forward.

When you get the appointment for the interview, start your research by reviewing the job description to identify your most relevant skills and experiences. Study the organization's web site to learn their mission statement, values, products, services, and customers. Compose stories that reflect your qualifications to meet their needs. Writing a script for yourself here would not hurt.

Targeted information enables you to concentrate on what the employer is looking for, eliminate extraneous anecdotes, and position yourself as a focused candidate who understands the employer's needs and priorities.

This is where you use the accomplishment statements we talked about earlier. Accomplishment statements allow you to PROVE what you can do. Proof makes you stand out as a great candidate.

4. Panel interviews

In a panel interview, two or more interviewers play off each other while taking turns asking you questions. This often is called a "tag team interview." The function is primarily to see how well you handle stress while facing two people *(some people call this a firing squad.)* A panel interview also measures how you interact with different people. Your panel could be future bosses, peers or even subordinates to the position for which you're interviewing.

This kind of interview, while more unusual, doesn't have to be more stressful.

Many times, you will not know you are going to be interviewed by a panel until you arrive, but the research and preparation you did for a one-on-one interview will be exactly what you need.

What will differ is your interview style. When you are asked a question, respond initially with good eye contact to the person who asked the question. As you speak, make eye contact with the other people in the room. Scan from one pair of eyes to the next, pausing briefly with each person. In other words, speak to the whole panel. As you finish your answer, focus back on the interviewer who asked the question. Shift your attention as each person asks you questions.

5. Informational interviews

This is more of a networking interview than a job interview, although you can apply the same techniques to job interviews. It differs considerably from other interviews because *you* make the appointment, usually *you* ask most of the questions, and *you* manage the process.

Here is how it works. Identify someone you think can offer information you need about your target industry and its trends. This is also a place to ask is there anybody else your interviewee knows who could give you more information.

Bring a list of the questions. Since you are the one initiating the conversation, be very considerate of time. This interview should last no longer than 30 minutes unless your contact begins asking you questions and engages you in a longer conversation.

All other interview etiquette applies. You know the drill: Be on time, dress appropriately, prepare, and write a thank you note for the person's time. In your note, offer your willingness to stay in touch and return the favor to them if they would like to hear the outcome of your research or the results of your network expansion.

We also recommend a follow-up letter after your thank you note, to let the person know you pursued a suggestion or contact your interviewee suggested. People appreciate knowing they helped you, and a follow-up note builds a networking relationship.

6. Peer group interviews

The simplest form of a group interview is a company presentation for a group of job candidates. Often, open discussion follows, with questions and answers. This gives the company a chance to observe how the candidates behave, interact, and possibly stand out among their peers.

Another form of a group interview is to invite employees to interview the candidate. This group is frequently made up of peers, but as companies become more sophisticated in their hiring practices and teamwork becomes a bigger issue, the group may include subordinates. In other words, the interviewers may end up working for you.

Now why on earth would a company do this? Involving employees in the selection process emphasizes the importance of the team. When employees are involved, they have a stake in the new hire's success. Personalities do count when it comes to collaborative, cooperative, and harmonious working relationships.

Supervisors, peers, and subordinates evaluate a prospective employee's skills and values differently. All these individual groups will be working with the new employee. Seeing candidates through different eyes provides a much clearer picture of how each new hire would fit into the open position.

Human resources professionals advocate group interviews because they believe it shortens transition times into the company. Being able to identify familiar faces and greet people who were part of the interview process makes starting a new job easier.

Also, employees are more adept at identifying specific skills needed for a position and they can respond meaningfully to an applicant's questions about the job. This is yet another screening process. Some people call it jumping through hoops; we say it is just more fish to fry.

When being interviewed by a group it is appropriate to ask for each person's name and job title. Write this information down, you will want to refer to it, and you will need it for thank you notes. Take the time to do this; you will be respected and remembered in a positive way for it.

The same preparation you would do for any interview applies here; do your homework.

Ask meaningful questions. It shows interest and enthusiasm for the job. Take your time, think through the answers to the questions carefully. The interviewers are looking for interpersonal, communication, and persuasion skills.

Because there are more and more candidates for a single job, some companies take group interviews to another level by simulating the work environment. For example, they might split the group into teams and give each a work-related hypothetical situation. The interviewers ask the teams to present their results in front of the group or job candidates present the team findings in the form of a personal presentation.

During group interviews, interviewers might closely observe and eavesdrop, ask and solicit questions from the candidate, take notes, and sometimes interject a twist or two, all to see how the candidate will respond. Although you are in a team, bet your best skillet you are being scrutinized.

Group interviewers might be looking to see who takes charge, how well he or she delegates tasks, and how other members react to his or her leadership.

They will also observe for:

- How you improvise or adapt to any situation
- How you handle stress
- Planning skills
- Involvement of team members
- Giving constructive criticism
- Accepting criticism, constructive or otherwise
- Focusing on resolving the issue at hand

Here are a couple of tips: It's better to be a leader than a follower. It's better to be an active participant than a passive observer. And the biggest advantage we have given you is telling you about this kind of interview in advance. It is becoming more and more common; being prepared and not surprised is the best strategy.

7. Internal interviews

An internal interview gives employees the opportunity to interview for jobs within their company, whether for a lateral move or a promotion. A good example is a claims adjuster handling worker compensation claims who wants to manage accident and health claims. The adjuster retains all benefits but changes departments, bosses, co-workers and work locations all within the same company.

All the usual interview etiquette applies, including writing a thank you note and dressing in interview attire, even if business casual is the dress code.

What is different here is how you apply. You usually apply through the human resources department *with the approval of your present boss* or with your present boss' recommendation. You may have discussed this move with your boss as part of your career development. **In any case, your boss must know of your interest and approve your request before you can interview.** Your boss may also know of a position and recommend you for a promotion. Do not make the mistake of going over your boss's head. It can be career suicide.

There are procedures for obtaining permission to change jobs. It is very important to follow them or you might never get a chance to move out of your department.

Another major difference is that your interviewer will have your most recent, or all of your performance reviews. Since you also have copies of your reviews, or you should have (as an employee of the company you are entitled to a copy of your reviews) there should be no surprises concerning your prior performance.

Is there is a category in which your performance was less than stellar? Be prepared to answer questions using your accomplishment statements.

Internal interviews are also different in that you are not an unknown entity. Your interviewer can get information about you informally via the company grapevine.

We suggest you get as much information about the job, the department, and the interviewer as possible before you request to interview. If you are unhappy where you are, moving to a different department may not solve your problem. Getting a new set of pots and pans will not necessarily make you a better cook. The key is always research and preparation.

8. Restaurant interviews and manners in general

We all know that some bosses will not hire an employee (especially one who will be involved in representing the company outside of the office) without taking them to lunch. *This is where you can make your mother proud!*

- Never order messy food.
- Order something in the price range of the host's selection.
- Never order alcohol, even if the host does.
- Put your napkin on your lap.
- Say please and thank you to not only your host, but to the food server as well.
- Remember that you start on the outside and work your way in with utensils. Your liquid is to your right and your solids are to the left.
- Elbows off the table.
- Never talk with your mouth full.
- Spoon soup away from you.
- Break a roll into pieces and eat a piece at a time.
- When you have finished eating, put your knife and fork to the "four o'clock position."

- When you leave, place your napkin on the table next to your plate.

Consider it a very good sign if you get an invitation to interview at a restaurant. Prospective employers will not spend money on you unless they are interested. Remember though; just like your mom told you table manners were important growing up, table manners are even more important now.

Another word or two about manners....

The number of people who lose out on jobs because of bad manners is staggering. We aren't just referring to table manners; let's start with the somewhat obvious statement that regardless of where you are in the job search or on the job, being rude is not acceptable. You don't get to pick and choose when to be nice and who you are nice to. Be respectful to everyone and then you will not have to worry about manners in an interview. That said, let us address a few times during the job search when your best manners need to be in the forefront.

An interview starts in the parking lot. Be watchful of signs marking off someone's spot. How many times have we heard the story about a candidate parking where he did not belong only to find out he took the interviewer's parking spot. This is not the best way to start the interview.

Also, do not litter. Be aware that the building has windows with people behind them. This is not the time to smoke and throw the butt in the parking lot.

By the way...remember the windows...the parking lot also is not the place to put on make-up or touch up with your electric shaver.

Everyone you meet as you enter the building has the potential to influence the hiring decision. There are many small companies, (your best target market) in which the owner's wife is the receptionist. Don't think she won't tell her husband if the candidate waiting for the interview is less than gracious or kind to her.

We know of a company in which, the Vice President of a company often goes down to the security desk to see how people respond to the check in process at the front desk. As we said, the interview begins in the parking lot.

We have already discussed thank you notes; keep in mind a thank you note is always appropriate for each and everyone who has helped you along the way. Do not underestimate the power of an executive assistant. We know one assistant who put the resume of a candidate on the top of the boss' mail each day for three days. He wrote a note that said "great candidate" on the top or the resume. This was in response to the candidate genuinely making him a part of his search, taking the time to make some chitchat, and being kind. The job candidate thinks acknowledging the assistant as an important person in the company helped to get him the second interview.

9. Video/teleconference interviews

Here again, you may not know you will be interviewing via Internet video until you arrive at the interview. Preparation is the same as for your other interviews. The only difference is the venue. Remember, even though you are videotaped, you do not have to be photogenic to get the job unless you are interviewing for a TV anchor position.

Having a piece of toilet paper on your face from a shaving nick or lipstick on your teeth will make you memorable in a less than complimentary way.

Smile, sit up, and lean forward slightly. Use good eye contact with the interviewer, not necessarily the camera; it will help if you can forget that you are on Candid Camera. This is no small feat. If you are not used to being on TV, this can throw even the most experienced interviewee. Admit you are nervous, it is natural, and you will be respected for acknowledging it.

If you have done all the necessary preparation, there is nothing more you can do except to sell yourself the same way you would in other types of interviews.

Information is power. No matter what type of interview, you never allow yourself to be surprised. The best way to do that is prepare well. Thorough preparation will give you a working knowledge of how to strategize any interview to succeed.

Now that you have been grilled and cooked to perfection, get ready to do the same for you dinner. Grill away

Speedy Salmon

Balsamic & Herb Lamb Chops

Steve's Onion Stacks

Cheese Fingers

Speedy Salmon

1 whole salmon fillet   1 c Shoyu Sauce
¼ c sugar   1 ½ c water
1 tbsp. fresh chopped ginger
4 cloves chopped garlic (or 4 tsp minced)
1 tsp. black pepper
2 stalks green onion (chopped) Cilantro
Olive Oil

Prepare marinade by mixing shoyu, sugar, and water. Add ginger, ½ of garlic, pepper and onions. Place salmon in mixture and marinade 2-4 hours.

Prepare sauce by heating ½ c oil, ½ of garlic, 1 Tbsp ginger. Cook until brown.

Grill fish 1-5 minutes on each side until it turns white. Place fish on platter; sprinkle with green onions and cilantro. Spoon sauce over fish.

Balsamic & Herb Grilled Lamb Chops

Ingredients for marinade:
1 tsp. dried rosemary (or 1 Tbsp fresh minced rosemary)
1 tsp. dried thyme (or 1 Tbsp fresh minced thyme)
1 tsp. dried basil (or 1 Tbsp. fresh minced basil)
2 tsp. minced garlic   1 Tbsp. olive oil   2 Tbsp. balsamic vinegar   1 Tbsp. Dijon mustard   Salt and Pepper
4 lamb chops

Place dried (or fresh) herbs and garlic in a small bowl and crush with fingers. Stir in olive oil, balsamic vinegar and mustard. Rub on lamb chops and set aside while grill or broiler is heating (approx. 15 minutes). Season chops with salt and pepper and grill (or broil) 4-5 minutes per side until medium rare.

Steve's Onion Stacks

8 (1/4-inch-thick) sweet onion slices (about 3 onions)
1/3 cup balsamic vinegar   1/4 cup olive oil   1 teaspoon salt
1/2 teaspoon freshly ground pepper
1 (8-ounce) package fresh mozzarella cheese,
cut into 4 (1/2-inch-thick) rounds
4 (1/2-inch-thick) fresh tomato slices (about 2 tomatoes)

Place onion slices in a single layer in a 13 x 9-inch baking dish. Stir together vinegar and next 4 ingredients. Pour over onion slices. Cover and chill 8 hours, turning once. Remove onions from dressing with a slotted spatula, reserving dressing. Grill onion slices, covered with grill lid, over medium-high heat (350 degrees to 400 degrees) 2 minutes on each side or until crisp-tender and golden. Layer half the grilled onion slices each with 1 slice of cheese, and on tomato slice. Grill onion stacks, covered with grill lid, over medium-high heat for 3 minutes or until cheese melts. Serve onion stacks with reserved dressing.

Cheese Fingers

4 baking potatoes; scrubbed
½ c fresh parmesan cheese
Salt & pepper
1 stick butter

Quarter potato lengthwise. Rub cut surfaces with butter: sprinkle generously with parmesan cheese, salt, and pepper. Put quarters together to re-form potato. Rub outside with butter. Wrap in foil. Roast in hot coals about 40 minutes, until tender… or bake in regular oven at 400° for 1 hour.

Chapter 6

How to Find the Jobs...Side Dishes

We have talked about networking as the best way to find a job....and truly, it is. However, there are still other ways to go about job search. We consider these ways to be 'side dishes' that go along with your chicken dinner and main course.

Using Newspapers and other Publications

The newspaper and other publications (online or paper) are great sources of information. They are particularly helpful to you in finding out what is going on in your industry.

Different sections of the newspaper highlight new industries and industries that are growing. Newspapers also recognize promotions and expansions. This is particularly true of local papers or trade publications, for example, in Chicago it's <u>Crain's Chicago Business</u>. Publications similar to Crain's in a specific geographical area are prime for best offerings for the job hungry reader.

Consult trade journals and other periodicals for opportunities, too. If you are a member of a particular industry, there are periodicals you review on a regular basis. Do not overlook these publications when searching for job openings and information about what companies are doing. You may also learn about conventions, seminars, and workshops. This can be a great way to find out where professionals like you are gathering. Many times, associations offer discounts to job seekers. This is a valuable way to meet a lot of people in one place in a short time.

When you find an article about a promotion, clip it, and mail it to the person. Include a congratulatory note and a message that you would love to be of service if they ever need help in their new position. (Remember the networking chapter idea?)

Along that same line, someone who has been promoted has likely left a previous position open. Could you fill that spot? Send a cover letter and resume or broadcast letter to the company that is expanding and explain how they could benefit from your expertise.

Don't over look obituaries. Quite often, the name of the company where the deceased worked is in the paper. A respectful cover letter expressing condolences would be appropriate. We had a client who read in the Sunday paper about a vice president of a local company who had passed away. Monday morning he wrote a card that was short but respectful to the president and dropped it off personally. With the card was a letter stating that whenever the president felt it was appropriate to interview candidates, he would like to be considered because he was familiar with the industry and could hit the ground running. The candidate was interviewed the next week and began the following week. No kidding.

Let's take a few minutes to dish about job ads (again online or on paper).

A job ad is a quick way to look at all types of positions within a company or geographical area. Before we go on, here is a fact: many jobs are not advertised. The ads that do advertise jobs also can help pinpoint industries and companies where there is employment activity. Often when the ad is printed, the job is already filled.

However, just reading the employment ads can give you a lot of information so keep checking the job ads. They will give you ideas on where to conduct your search. Remember; we advocate trying every method to find a job, and to keep trying them until you land what you are looking for. (Are you keeping track of how many times we say this?)

Companies usually follow a four-step process for finding candidates for a specific job.

1. The hiring manager knows there will be an opening. Either someone is leaving, fired, or there is more work than available personnel can handle.
2. The hiring manager discusses the opening with human resources and a decision is made about how the job is filled, what the salary range should be, education level of the candidate, experience, etc.
3. The job is posted in-house. Many companies offer a bonus to employees if they refer a candidate that is eventually hired.

4. The job is posted online and in print publications, and thundering herds of candidates appear--all looking at the same job you are.

Notice how many people know about the job before it is published anywhere. This is why networking works. If an employee told you about a job, you applied and got it, you have landed a job even before it was advertised. This is the beauty of relationship building and networking.

Companies receive hundreds, sometimes thousands of responses. But don't give up, sometimes people do find jobs through newspaper ads. The key to success is to increase your odds by standing out, particularly if you apply for a newspaper ad or on-line ad.

Here are some ways to distinguish yourself:
- Learn as much as possible about the company before responding to the ad.
- Use your cover letter to answer every point mentioned in the ad. See Chapter 3 for some great cover letter examples.
- Look for a good fit, but don't expect to match exactly. If the ad mentions six requirements and you have three, go for it. What do you have to lose?

The ads we read online or in newspapers describe the employer's ideal candidate. Many employers use the website called ONET (http://online.onetcenter.org/) to determine what to write in a job description. ONET is the online *Dictionary of Occupational Titles.* Prior to reviewing the want ads, take some time to review ONET and make certain your resume has the *keywords* you need to connect with the prospective employer.

- Read the entire ad. You might call yourself a materials manager but the ad for your perfect job, the job you exactly fit, is a logistics expert. So, what do you do? Change your language. (This may seem obvious, remember we have more than 50 years of experience, we know to many it is obvious and we also know to many more it isn't.)
- Read the body of the ad, not just the title.
- Read openings in different industries to see how your skills could transfer.
- Read local papers, Sunday papers, and trade publications.
- Send your resume electronically. Follow up in a day or two to make certain the prospective employer received your resume.
- Once you apply online, send your resume the next day by hard copy.

- Follow up ten days later with another copy. If you were overlooked the first time, there will be fewer people sending resumes later, and you could make it to the top of the shorter pile this time.

Though searching online ads and newspapers is an inefficient way to look for a job, it should not be overlooked. Why? Because you never know what method is going to be the one to get you the interview. You have to try everything and keep on trying until you land the job. 60 to 80% of available jobs are not listed in any ad. Reason suggests you should spend 60 to 80 per cent of your time looking for jobs through networking. What do you do with the rest of your time? Divvy it up talking recruiters, attending job fairs, and perusing other ads (all kinds of ads).

The best time to look at ads is when you cannot network. Early mornings, later in the evening and weekends are best. Use work hours (9 to 5) to hit the phones to generate more job leads, set up face-to-face meetings, or go networking in a variety of places.

Salary History

So, there you are looking at the ads and you find the perfect job. And then, the scary part: salary history required! Those nosy job ads. Have you ever **not** sent a resume because the ad said, "salary history required"?

Here's another thing to try – send your resume anyway. In your cover letter, address the fact that this ad has requested salary history. You really have to acknowledge that you have omitted a specific request. Address the omission by indicating, "I am sure we can come to a mutually beneficial agreement regarding compensation."

If you have not applied online, generally when you arrive for an interview you have to complete an application. Usually, in the application, there will be a category that requests your salary requirements. The written directions may also include "This application is not complete unless every question is answered." Hmmm… Salary History. Uh-oh. Now what?

We advise our clients to complete this section with words such as, "Open, flexible, or negotiable." If possible, at the bottom of the application, write, "I will be glad to discuss this in an interview." You are still not giving anything away, and the organization doesn't know if they can afford you or not. If the employer looks at your resume and believes you can solve a problem or make a profit, he will interview you.

Now that isn't going to work if you are applying online. An online application may not allow you to advance unless you fill out all of the information. Once again, be prepared before you start filling out the application. Knowledge of what the salary range is for your position in your industry is important. Knowledge of what they may be offering will help you decide how to state your salary. (Doing your research homework on this company will help you here.)

There are times when you have to divulge your prior salary. If you really feel pressed, use a range. Vary the range to indicate you are flexible.

When you consider what number to put down for yourself, do you include your benefits and bonus as salary? Yes, if it is to your advantage. No, if it is not. How do you know? Once again Preparation – know the facts. Sometimes including that number puts you way above the usual range. You don't ever want to lie, but sometimes you don't want to give all of the information. The ONET website http://online.onetcenter.org and www.salary.com are great sources of information regarding salary. There is more about salaries and negotiating coming up in chapter seven.

Using social networks in your job search

Another side dish to a job search is social networking. Social networking is one of the latest and greatest techniques for finding the right position since sliced bread. www.LinkedIn.com, www.Facebook.com, www.MySpace.com, www.Twitter.com, and www.Plaxo.com are just a few options. More are emerging by the minute. How do they fit in with job search?

Simply put, social networking sites are web-based services that allow you to expand your business and/or social contacts by making connections to other individuals electronically. This concept is based on the 'six degrees of separation' - the idea that any two people on the planet could make contact through a chain of no more than five individuals. Social networking establishes Internet communities that help people make contacts in their network but that they otherwise would be unlikely to make.

For this discussion we are going to discuss just two sites, www.LinkedIn.com and www.Facebook.com.

Here's how it works: You join a site and invite people you know to join you as a friend or business colleague. In turn, those people invite their contacts to join, who then invite *their* contacts to join them and so on. In theory, anyone can make contacts through someone they have a connection with to any of the people *that* person is connected to…truly, it could go on forever!

www.LinkedIn.com is one of the most popular networking sites. Currently, it is the more professional or business-oriented of the social networking sites. Many people have found jobs using LinkedIn because of its organization and the safeguards that help you navigate securely. LinkedIn is a place to find and leverage professional opportunities throughout your career.

It helps you:

- Present yourself and your professional capabilities
- Find and reconnect with colleagues and classmates
- Leverage powerful tools to find and reach the people you need
- Build a powerful network of trusted professionals
- Discover professional relationships and opportunities
- Tap into inside connections and information
- Get an edge that gives you a competitive advantage

Here are some tips to use www.LinkedIn.com to find a job:

1. Create a profile that includes employment, education, industry your web site.
2. In your profile, include all your industry keywords and skills so when an employer does a search, you pop up.
3. Consider adding a photo but make sure it looks professional. You don't want the funny picture of you in a chef's hat.
4. Build a network by connecting with people you know. The more connections you have, the more opportunities you will discover.
5. Ask for recommendations from people you have worked with or for.
6. Make recommendations for people you know and have worked with or for
7. Search for jobs by using the job search section to find listings.
8. Review the answers section and respond to questions. Also, ask a question that can highlight your visibility.
9. Remember to use LinkedIn daily during your search to look at profiles, invite new connections, and search for companies.

www.Facebook.com is a site that allows you to connect with friends and family. It is really more of a friend/social site. You can create and customize your profile with photos, videos, and information about yourself. Friends can browse your profile and the profiles of other friends. You exchange messages on their pages. Sound like fun? Well, it is but, there is a down side to social networking. Remember that crazy New Year's party a few years ago and the friendly party pal who kept bringing you margaritas? Seems that a camera was nearby and someone recorded your wild reveling and posted it on Facebook!

Guess what? Employers are now using social networking sites to review possible job candidates. A recent study found that 77 percent of recruiters run searches of job seekers on social networking sites and 35 percent of them say they have eliminated a candidate based on information they found!

Employers and recruiters report numerous instances when they were having a difficult time choosing between two candidates. Then they did a search of the social networking sites and a less than flattering photo of one of the candidates was found. We heard another story about a candidate who told a prospective employer that she was currently working for a company, yet on www.MySpace.com, she revealed how much fun it was to be unemployed. Big surprise, the company made the decision to hire somebody else.

And another story, a recruiter went to a candidate's website and found off color jokes and racial slurs. You have to ask yourself: "What were they thinking"? That one mistake will leave a terrible impression they will have no chance to correct.

Realize that the Internet has a long, long memory and you must manage your online image whether you are searching for a job or not. The risks don't stop once you are hired. Postings never ever go away.

It doesn't matter who owns the computer. If you make an entry at home from a personal e-mail address and use that for a social networking site at work, any published content that addresses professional matters written on the site can be grounds for termination or a lawsuit. **To repeat, the Internet never forgets.**

Writing something that is inflammatory or breaches a confidentiality agreement for the company is even more serious for the employee. Anybody who looks for it can find this information. Now employers are all looking.

Always think about what you say in emails, always. Assume you can get in trouble for everything you say. Err on the side of caution, your boss may be following your Tweets, viewing Your Wall, or looking at any other form of public comment on a social web site.

Yet another story, benefit from this experience and watch what you write.

> Susan found her dream job working as an attorney for a high-profile practice in Chicago. As a native of southern California, Susan put up a profile on MySpace to meet new people. She felt she was careful and did not give any information she thought was too personal or could be intrusive.
>
> Time passed, Susan made friends and started going out to sporting events, concerts and other events. One Friday, Susan called in sick to spend a day with her new friends, going on a last minute trip to an out-of-town concert. That weekend, completely without her knowledge, one of her friends posted a few pictures of Susan along with a message saying 'We should call in sick more often.'
>
> Coincidence would have it that Susan's boss uses MySpace regularly and has his own profile. Guess what happened? Of course, he found the pictures…name, dates, and all. Susan lost her job.

Susan learned the hard lesson of how close we are to each other through social networking and the Internet. You can't control what information is out there, but you can control what *you* put out there.

Beware, the trend is growing. Remember that six degrees of separation may only be three degrees on the Internet. To protect yourself, keep in mind that nothing is private. Do not post anything on any sites you would not want a prospective employer to discover, because they will.

Revealing photos, inappropriate language, tasteless jokes, and racial slurs reflects badly on your character. Remember to be discreet. Check out the social networking site and consider keeping your profile private. It will not be available to the whole world, only to the friends you choose. The Internet is *your* permanent record!

Also stay on top of the situation. Check your profile regularly and see what comments have been posted. Search engine yourself and see what is out there about you. If there is something negative, take action to deal with it before someone uses it against you. In other words, make sure you know all there is to know about yourself. Use social networking to your advantage.

Working with a recruiter

The recruiter is a searcher and a matchmaker. He has to search for job openings and then match a candidate to fill the job.

Recruiters' primary function is to gauge a candidate's fit for the position and for the company's culture. Recruiters make commissions by how well they make this fit. A recruiter is paid in a variety of different ways depending on their agreements with prospective employers.

There are two kinds of recruiting organizations: contingency and retained. The difference between the two is how they are paid. When a contingency firms place a job candidate, they are make money. That is the only result that earns them compensation. The client or hiring company pays a retained firm in advance.

Why is this important, since the hiring company pays in both cases?

Retained firms have both an area of specialization and a big network of contacts. Because they specialize, over time the firm develops a reputation for successfully placing strong candidates in specific industries. This is true even in difficult economic times and for hard-to-fill positions. Retained firms with good reputations usually work with select clients.

To make any money, contingency firms must work with more clients; both job seekers and hiring firms. As a job seeker, you have to be careful if you are working with a contingency firm. The firm could submit your resume without your permission or knowledge. If you decide to work with a contingency recruiter, put it in writing to the recruiter that your resume is not submitted without your consent.

Remember, the contingency firm is working with many candidates and hiring companies. They are competing with other recruiting firms. This type of recruiting firm is moving faster to fill the position. Contingency recruiters frequently do not give you, the job seeker, the name of the firm where they submit your credentials. Again, this is a competitive issue because if you know the name of the company, you might submit your resume on your own. If you're hired, the recruiter gets no commission. This is why he wants to play it close to the chest.

Because they are paid in advance, retained search firms tend to go slower filling positions. Their interviewing is more in-depth, for both the job seeker and the prospective employer. And since they have been paid, they don't have to worry about losing their fee, so the retained recruiter will tell the job candidate as much as they know about the job and the company. It serves their interests to have informed candidates who can research and do their own homework, interview successfully, and increase their odds of being hired.

For the job seeker, working with a retained firm means your search might take longer. However, if you take our advice, recruiters are one more tool in the job search. They are useful, but we encourage you to try every method and keep trying them all until you find the right job.

(How many times have we said this? In this case, repetition is good.) Recruiters can be an excellent tool.

Following is a list of different types of recruiters that can help you figure out who you want to work with and why. Ask the recruiter what type of firm he works for; it will make life easier for you.

Types of Recruiters:

Corporate recruiter: A corporate recruiter is usually an employee of the organization that is hiring. The employee can be salaried or paid an hourly rate. Tracking and reporting quotas are part of their job description.

Human Resource Generalist: In addition to doing usual HR functions, a generalist will take the role of internal recruiter to fill job openings. They are salaried employees but often receive bonuses for successful recruiting.

Researchers: Researchers function as explorers and screeners by identifying potential candidates and then turning them over to a recruiter for closer review and interviewing. Either independent recruiters or corporate recruiters can employ them. Employer's policy determines compensation.

Agency recruiter: An agency recruiter is paid by commission, although sometimes agencies pay a small base salary. The agency charges the hiring company a percentage of the starting salary for every position the agency fills. The percentage of salary varies depending on the position and the state of the economy of the region. In general, the fee is 25 per cent to 35 percent of the annual starting salary of the new hire.

Independent Recruiters: Independent recruiters are self-employed agents. The commission they make varies according to the salaries of the positions they fill. If they do not fill a position, they make nothing.

Contract Recruiter: A contract recruiter is temporarily hired by the company to fill a specific position. Compensation is usually hourly based.

Independent Recruitment Agencies or Executive Search Firms: Organizations like this usually work on executive positions or hard-to-fill positions. These agencies are paid 30 per cent to 35 per cent of the annual starting salary for the position they are trying to fill. They operate on a retainer and usually receive compensation whether they fill the position or not.

Working with a recruiter can be a good opportunity to gain insight into your chosen industry. They know the trends and the market. Another plus is the higher the position's salary, the more the recruiter makes. This is often a strong incentive for the recruiter to get you the highest possible salary. However, remember that the employer pays the recruiter, and your recruiter is building sustained and profitable relationships with employers, his future depends on it.

The bottom line here is, the recruiter wants to represent and place good qualified workers, he/she also wants to keep a solid relationship with the employer, and the recruiter wants to make money. Reflect on this information when it comes time to talk salary.

Here are a few tips and issues to take into account when working with or considering working with a recruiter:

- As a job seeker, a recruiting firm, no matter which type of firm you work with, should never charge you.
- You are working with an individual recruiter not the agency. You must build and sustain a compatible relationship with the recruiter. If you do not have a good relationship with him, you are less likely to get in the door of the company, no matter how good or experienced you are.
- Ask lots of questions. You are working with this person as your representative or advocate; find out if they are the right person to help you in your job search.
- Look for a specialist. Recruiters specialize; they know the job market and trends in a particular area (technology for example). Stay with an industry specialist.
- Stay local with your recruiter if you want to stay in the area. They will be familiar with area industry trends, communities, commuter lines and sometimes-even school districts. If you want to move, find a recruiter in the target geographical area where you want to work for all the same reasons.
- Be honest with your recruiter. He will be your advocate; it is his responsibility to place you. The recruiter wants to do a good job to build customer relationships. Don't let this individual down by overstating your experience or expertise.
- Provide all the information the recruiter asks for quickly and comprehensively.
- Know what you are worth and the least amount of compensation you would consider; don't waste the recruiter's time or yours.

- Always check the facts; be sure you are getting the correct details from all parties.
- If you get an offer and you are happy, great, take the job. If you are not, ask the recruiter to negotiate a better deal for you. It is often part of the recruiter's responsibilities.
- Working with a contingency recruiter might give you a slightly faster result simply because the recruiter has more clients.
- Never, never, let a recruiter talk you into a job in which you are not suited or doesn't feel right. The company, its culture, the location, your responsibilities, benefits, advancement opportunities are all part of the job. In the end, you are the one going to a job each day. It is your life, not the recruiter's, so decide carefully.

Working and interviewing with a recruiter is just like a job interview, so prepare, and anticipate questions and answers. Remember; the recruiter earns his money by making a good fit. Your recruiter will need good information to present you in a way that will land you the job you want and give the employer a good employee. This is in addition to giving your recruiter a good commission and a solid relationship for future business.

When you meet and begin getting to know your recruiter, be prepared with the following information.

1. Complete *current* compensation details. Your recruiter needs to know the exact structure of your compensation package. That is base salary, bonuses, stock options and a list of benefits. This might not be what you want, but it is what you have right now or if you are unemployed what you did have

2. Type of commute. Commuting is a quality of life issue and discussing it is important. A ten-minute drive against traffic is very different from taking the car to a train and then walking five blocks from the station to the job location. Your recruiter should bring up the differences in distance and what it means to you. Moreover, you should think about that, too.

3. What is the difference between what you want and what you have? Most people don't change jobs just for the sake of changing jobs. They change because something is missing in what they are doing now and what they would like to be doing. This disparity is called *"position differential."* Your recruiter will want to know yours *"position differential"* no matter what your present or past employment record.

Think about what you want or don't want in your next position. Everybody wants something. Know what it is for you, maybe it's several things. Know what your top priority is. You should have five things that are "need to haves" not "nice to haves." Be able to state them clearly to the recruiter.

4. How do you work best, alone or on a team? Your recruiter will know the company's basic philosophy and the way the hiring manager asks questions about teams and teaming to see how you will fit into the culture. Remember; your style is as important as your substance and experience to your recruiter. If you are a better project manager than a team leader, tell your recruiter that.

5. What are your over all strengths and weaknesses? Know your strong points and your limitations. The recruiter will try to identify them to define not only how you will do the job but also how you will fit into the organization. Just as in the real job interview, achievement statements are important here.

6. How many recruiters are you working with? Some candidates work with several. If you are interviewing with a company, it is a good idea to let all your recruiters know the name of the company. They might want to hurry a hiring manager along if they know they are competing for you. On the other hand, some companies work with several recruiters, too. Keeping everybody on the same page is a very good idea for the job seeker.

7. Know what it will take to close the deal. This is more specific than knowing what you want. For example, if you want more money as an absolute "must have," how much more money will it take to accept the position? If you want to work on different projects, what projects will it take to get you to move? If your recruiter knows this information, he will be a better advocate for you.

8. Be prepared with solid information regarding your capabilities. Your recruiter has to trust that you have been straight with him. This information is important to get you the best fit for both you and the organization. Once again, if you have solid experience, list it for the recruiter. Often, documentation from a discrete former co-worker or someone who knows your work can be very useful to verify your capabilities.

9. Be able to tell the recruiter what culture fits you the best. You may not be the type that can work for a startup company that has its office in a garage. Maybe you enjoy a slower pace and more structured atmosphere. Tell your recruiter that. If you are a round peg trying to

force yourself into a square hole, it will probably not work well for you or your recruiter.

If working with a recruiter appeals to you, one resource to help you find a recruiter is *The Directory of Executive Recruiters*. Networking with other job seekers for the names of reputable recruiters is also a good option and, of course, explore on your own. Once again, you are looking for a fit, someone you trust and can work with well.

During your job search, you may come across the following agencies. This is a way to make sure you know the service is being offered to you as well as knowing how an agency can help you.

Outplacement Agencies: Outplacement agencies are companies that assist terminated corporate employees to re-enter the job market. They receive payment by the organization on a per-person basis and on the different services included in the termination package. Services can in a package or a la carte and range from helping a candidate write a resume to providing administrative and research services during job searches. Outplacement agencies do not find a job for you; they help prepare you to find your own job.

Temporary to Permanent Contract Agencies: These organizations hire and pay employees to perform services for companies. They mark up the contracted employee's hourly rate to make their profit. The length of service can vary from a day to several months.

These agencies frequently offer jobs that become permanent. Consider temporary opportunities very seriously. They offer a wonderful chance to see how the company works and the company gets a chance to see how the employee works. If one or the other isn't happy, the contract is not renewed. Nobody is fired; the company just gets another candidate. Taking a temporary job is an excellent option during the job search.

Job fairs

Is your glass half-full or half empty?

We hear great stories of people who have attended job fairs and met wonderful people and we have heard just as many people say they are a waste of time. We tend to look at the half-full glass. Getting out and meeting people is always better than sitting home watching TV or staring at your computer screen. A job fair is another place to start uncovering possibilities.

You can explore career opportunities with a variety of companies at a single location. Job fairs are a great way to research companies and practice interviewing and networking techniques. You never know whom you are going to meet for the first time.

Let's do some strategic thinking to learn how to make the most of the job fair opportunity.

To get started, get information about the job fair first-hand. All major event holders have corporate web sites. When you find out when and where the fair will be, go to the event sponsor and check which companies or vendors will participate. Download a map of the event.

Think about your research as a two-part process.

First, determine what types of positions will be featured. Some fairs show case specific industries or career functions. Make sure they feature the type of positions in which you are interested. Or not?

You might want to go to this job fair for the practice of doing a quick spot interview. Practice makes perfect. It doesn't hurt to mosey around a job fair just to be curious or go to support a buddy who is going to look for a job in his field. Any networking time out there is not wasted.

Second, review the list of participating companies and check their locations on your map. Go to their corporate web sites to learn about their culture, mission/vision statements, number of employees, products and services, benefit packages, their location, all the stuff you look for in target companies. Make a list of the companies that interest you most.

Once you have a list of companies and positions, send an email. You will have to do some research to find an email contact. You can always call human resources, that department usually manages career fairs for large corporations. Your email message should say you would be attending and look forward to meeting them.

Plan your chat with a company representative. Know enough about the company that you can give them a quick reason why this interaction should go to the next step: an interview for the position you want. At the event, try to get a business card and the name of the hiring manager for the positions the company wants to fill.

Don't be afraid to visit companies outside your industry. Even if your research suggests they offer nothing for you, this is a chance to make a contact. There is no risk. Do it. It is simply good practice and keeps you on your toes with your thirty-second introduction. You never know who will you meet and who that person knows. And it can be stimulating to give your job search a little jolt.

Go dressed for an interview, although make sure you wear comfortable shoes. You will do a lot of walking and you don't want to be limping around halfway through the event. Remember; you have only one chance to make a good first impression. Use this chance.

Bring tons of resumes and business cards and give them out. Collect cards from everyone, even fellow job seekers. Review the business card section in the networking chapter. Allow yourself ample time. The first day of a two or three day fair is always the best, and mornings are better than afternoons, everybody gets more tired in the afternoon.

You know which companies will be there, and you emailed the ones that interest you. Organize your time to be most effective. If the event is large, get a map when you arrive, check the map you downloaded against the new one. More companies may have been added or their location may have changed. You don't want to miss one that could be a target company for you.

Before you hit the companies that interest you, do a warm up. We know you rehearsed your thirty-second speech, now you have an audience, go perform. Visit some companies that might not be at the top of your list, talk to people, mingle a little, and get comfortable before the big debut. Warming up is always good. Then you will be ready to talk with companies at the top of your interest list.

If you engage someone at a company of interest in a good conversation, write a follow-up thank you note, even if it's for a brief interview. Email it that night so your name will be fresh in the interviewer's mind the next day. Then in a week, follow up with another note later in the week or the following week.

The day after the job fair, email each person that gave you a card. Tell them it was great meeting them and remind them what you are looking for. If they are job seekers too, mention that you will be keeping your eyes and ears open to help them. And then do just that. If you hear of something to help someone else, well, you know that drill. You will have nurtured your network, and now someone is going to be looking for leads for you in places you may never go yourself.

Consider a job fair an opportunity to do a mini-interview.

Try this approach:

- Since most people working the job fair for a company will be wearing a name tag, approach them with a smile, a firm hand shake, good eye contact and say, "Rich, what skills or characteristics would the ideal candidate (name the position you want) need to have to work for your company? Then use that information to sell yourself.

- "Let me tell you a little about my great qualifications." (Thirty second summary)
- Answer questions directly, concisely and politely.
- Express interest in the job, if, of course, you have interest.
- Ask Rich how he would rate your credentials compared to any other candidates they are considering.
- Ask, "What do I need to do to get an invitation to your company for an in depth interview?"
- All of this should take less than five minutes, unless Rich asks you questions and pursues the interview. Do not push to talk longer. Rich job is to recruit candidates, let him do his job.

Be sure you get Rich's card and, of course, do the follow up, just as you would for any interview.

Remember that an important aspect of a job fair is to gain exposure to other people, those with jobs, and those who are looking. Using your time effectively can help you get more referrals and information about companies. (Try everything and keep trying everything until you get that job.)

We have discussed many of the side dishes associated with search. Now whip up a few of your own to go with your main plate special!

Gorgonzola Cheese Baked Potatoes

Browned Carrots

Brussels Sprouts Milanese

Stuffed Tomatoes

Gorgonzola-Cheese Baked Potatoes

4 medium red potatoes, scrubbed
½-cup sour cream
3 Tablespoons crumbled Gorgonzola or blue cheese
Freshly ground pepper to taste
Snipped fresh chives optional

Pierce potatoes in several places. Place on microwave-safe plate, cook on high power until tender about 10 to 14 minutes, rotating quarter-turn after 5 minutes. Let stand 2 minutes.
Stir together sour cream, cheese, and pepper in small bowl. Split potatoes in half; place dollop of sour cream mixture on each. Sprinkle with chives.

Browned Carrots

1 lb baby carrots
1 stick real butter
Brown Sugar
Salt and pepper
Chopped parsley

Wash carrots and cut them into 3" lengths, then downward in thin slices, then each slice into strips.
Drop into boiling water, salted, and simmer until tender. If finely cut, this should not take over 25 or 30 minutes.
Put a tablespoon of butter in the frying-pan, and when very hot, add the drained carrots. Dredge lightly with salt and pepper, and a little sugar, and fry until lightly colored.
Sprinkle with chopped parsley, and serve.

Brussels Sprouts Milanese

1 lb fresh Brussels sprouts, steamed until bright green; but not mushy.
¾ cup (3 ounces each) each of grated Swiss and parmesan cheese, combined.
2 tbsp butter, melted
¼ tsp salt
Dash of pepper
1 tsp lemon juice
Place sprouts in buttered 1 qt baking dish. Sprinkle with cheese mixture. Blend butter, salt, pepper and lemon juice and pour over the sprouts. Bake at 350° 20 minutes, until lightly browned

Ma's Stuffed Tomatoes

6 medium-sized tomatoes   1 c cubed stuffing
¼ c diced onion   2 chopped celery stalks
1 tbsp poultry seasoning   ¼ c parmesan cheese
¼ c melted butter
¼ c chopped cooked ham or sausage (optional)
12 strips of mozzarella cheese
Dash of sugar

Wash tomatoes. Cut off stems and scoop out inside. Place 'insides' in separate bowl.
Rub a dash of sugar around the inside of each tomato.
Mix stuffing with insides of tomatoes. Add onion, celery and poultry seasoning. Mix gently and add parmesan cheese, melted butter and meat. Mix well and stuff tomato loosely.
Bake about ½-hour at 325°. Add mozzarella strips on top and bake a few minutes more.

Chapter 7

Getting the Offer and the Money... Ready for Dessert?

So up to this point, you have been doing everything right. You have a stellar resume. You have networked into a successful interview. We have coached you on how to answer all the tough questions, and Mr. Interviewer asks, "Well, Jack, how much money are we talking about here? How much will it take for you to accept this job?" This is the question you have been waiting for and dreading at the same time. Is it time to celebrate? No, not yet.

Ahhhhhhhh…..how do you get the money you want, keep your hold on the job, and not give yourself away for too little?

First, let's make sure you develop a sound idea of how much you are worth. Once again, doing your homework is vital. We have some research recommendations: www.jobstar.org is one good site that offers a comprehensive research guide to online salary surveys for lots of different occupations. Another site, www.salary.com makes statistics and data user friendly and easy to understand. We like this site because they work to keep it current, so your information is in real time markets. Our last favorite, www.careerjournal.com is the Wall Street Journal's site. It has useful information if you use the link, "Salaries for Industry." It links you to salaries, articles, and jobs that are in demand. These are just a few. There are more, look for them. It is up to you to know what jobs in your industry are worth and even more importantly, what you are worth.

So, prepare, prepare, prepare. (Sound familiar?) Get all the information you need to get a top salary for the job you want. Information will also help you decide what you are willing to accept. Remember, you will be hired to help this company make a profit. That means selling more products, making more widgets, providing a better service. Whatever the job function's responsibilities, you must become an asset to help this company make more money. Part of your interviewing strategy is to let Mr. Interviewer know how much additional profit you are likely to create. You have to make more for the company than you cost; it's as simple as that. In addition, you must be fair and competitive. We advocate placing your salary request in the middle of the applicable range.

You know that timing is everything in life. Effectively answering the salary question depends on when salary discussion comes in the interview. We coach our clients to put off responding directly to the money question until later in the interview. We suggest saying something like, "It's really too early to discuss salary. I think we both want the pay to be fair, so let's talk about what responsibilities I will handle and what value I can bring to your company."

This way, you have been polite without revealing how much you want. You have steered the conversation back to the job and your responsibilities. You have not spoken the money figure first. This is one of the most important strategies of a job interview and a key to landing the job. Most advisors will say: He who talks about money first loses. While this is not universally true, it is generally the case, and we believe it's good advice too.

There is another way to understand the whole salary negotiation process. Personalize it. Use the impact on your family finances as an example.

You know how much money you have to spend each month for utilities, clothes, food, etc. Balancing your household money is challenging but it is under control, there is just enough money for everything. Just enough money for everything but there isn't much more. Then the stove begins acting funny. The temperature gauge is off. You start thinking that maybe you'll have to shuffle your money to afford a new stove.

Then the stove gets worse. The oven no longer turns on and a burner doesn't work. You know meals are not going to be so terrific at your house, even with our recipes. So, though you know it will stretch your monthly budget, you start looking at appliance ads.

Notice, your monthly money has not increased. You're just now thinking about allocating it differently. You have moved from thinking all your money has been assigned, to adjusting your thinking, to starting to investigate the purchase of a new stove.

You begin to think that over time, the new stove will save you money because it will be more energy efficient, the meals will sure be better, and there will be cake in your house again. You might even start to think if you spend a little more and buy the best, you will not only be helping the environment, you'll be eating out less and saving even more money. You decide that the new stove will pay for itself in a few years with the savings in utility and restaurant bills alone. You make what then appears to be the right decision. You make the decision to buy the new stove.

Simply put, in deciding to buy a new stove, you have gone from being convinced you couldn't afford the appliance, to doing an evaluation of your life style, to concluding the stove will pay for itself, particularly if you buy a really good one.

The employer is thinking along the same lines when he begins considering hiring you. Mr. Interviewer may first think: "I can't afford him at that salary." Then after some interviewing: "Hey, he seems like a really smart, savvy man, he has to work for us. And then, I'm convinced he'll help make us more money than we are making now." And as in most things, profitability prevails, "I want to hire him."

All the employer has to figure out now is a way to afford you. If he is really sold on you, he will. Just as in your personal life, you found the money to buy the stove; he'll find the money to hire you.

This is why it pays to *postpone any salary discussions until you get an offer for the job*. You must sell yourself to fit the need the employer has so he will believe he can afford you.

Let's go back to a personal example. Think about how salary negotiation might apply to your own stove shopping experience. Say you've searched in several appliance stores for that new stove. You find just what you want, but when you ask ABC sales clerk how much it costs he says, "I know you're shopping, so before you decide to buy anywhere else, please come back and see me first." (He does did not give you a price, but holds out the hope that he will turn out be your best deal.)

So you shop some more and find another stove for $800, but you remember ABC sales clerk asked that you come back and check his price before buying. Wouldn't you go back? We would. We'd almost have to. The clerk didn't give a price, but encouraged you to investigate. He got you interested and hopeful enough to go back to see what that price might be.

If you hold salary negotiations until after you've established your value in the employer's eyes (after you've sold yourself) the same holds true. Mr. Interviewer is going to check back with you after the company decides exactly what it wants and what it's worth to them and who (YOU) is the best candidate to fill those expectations.

Then, if what you're asking for in salary is what the company decides hiring you is worth to them, it's a done deal. Matching your skills with what the employer needs is the whole point to interviewing and, of course, the salary negotiation process.

So, if Mr. Interviewer asks before the job offer: "Just what salary are you looking for?" Here are some polite and appropriate responses.

(1) "I am sure we can come to a good compensation agreement if we both decide I am the right person for your company."

(2) "Salary? Well, so far, the expectations and responsibilities for this job are things I am comfortable doing. I know you would pay a fair compensation for them, right? (*Of course, he will say yes, who would say they do not pay a fair wage.*) So let's not discuss salary until you are sure you want me. What other challenges and responsibilities does this position have?"

(3) "I see the salary issue is back in our conversation, maybe we should talk about why we need to discuss it now?"

(4) "For now, let's not worry about salary. I feel certain I will be a valuable addition to your organization, but let's just make sure your position and my abilities are a good fit." Frequently this comment will allow the interviewer to rest a little easier knowing you are interested in working for him and just want to learn more about the job.

We recommend saying these phrases in front of a mirror to inspire confidence and ease in your delivery. Before the interview, repeat the words until you feel comfortable saying them. We recommend a mock interview for salary negotiations. Try this conversation with your career coach or a colleague to give you practice and confidence.

The truth is, talking about money and salary is difficult for most people. Talking about what are worth is difficult for most people. We strongly encourage practicing here. It will give you confidence to say things you may find difficult.

And, there are many other ways to say the same thing, play with our examples to make them your own. Just as in recipes, adding your own spice makes the dish uniquely yours. Here, it's the same thing.

At this point, you talked to several people in the company and each time the "S" word is mentioned, you successfully diverted the conversation onto another relevant subject.

But what if you really get pushed to give your 'number'?

Go back to the research you did on what you are worth and combine it with research on the industry you are interviewing with and come up with a range…just a simple range. "I am looking at $52,000 to $63,000 a year, but I am open to discussion." Above all, do not start actually negotiating for the job at this point

At last, you have been offered the job.

Let's assume everything about the job fits and you are willing to accept it, but *if* and only *if*, the salary is right. What's next? Here is yet another place where having done your homework will pay off. You know the least you can accept and still make a living. You know what you would like to be paid and what the "market rate" are for this job.

In offering you a salary, Mr. Interviewer gives you a range (e.g., "We've budgeted between $90,000 and $120,000 for this position".) You repeat the top figure in the range ("120,000") and stop! Put a pensive look on your face and say nothing for about ten to thirty seconds. Literally, count off the seconds in your mind. Use that silent time to mentally review your salary requirements and decide how close the top number is to what you can accept.

Note: You repeat the top number in the range, suggesting who would ever accept something lower than the top figure. No, you repeat that top number for effect. This opens the negotiation. Our experience has shown that most of the time, when the employer mentions a range, he is thinking the low end, and most probably, you are thinking the high end.

The most common result of the money negotiation in this example is that Mr. Interviewer quickly raises the anti. He might say something like, "XX may not sound like much, and we could go YY for someone with your capabilities and experience."

As you might already know, silence is hard. It can be intimidating. It is often uncomfortable, (but uncomfortable only for those without a strategy; not you, you are using the silence to your advantage.). You are evaluating and planning how to respond, and you did your homework. You know what your numbers are. This knowledge will make what could be an uncomfortable silence only uncomfortable for the other person. This is exactly what you want in the negotiation.

Take your time. Fall back on the homework you did. Your research shows the most reasonable amount you can get based on the market, your skills, experience, etc., and the lowest number you would be willing to accept for this job. Compare these numbers to your offer. This is what you are thinking in that silence.

When you are ready to respond, what do you say? Well, you say the truth, whatever that is for you.

If you think that figure is it, give an emphatic, "yes." If it is acceptable, say it is acceptable. If it is not what you expected, you can say that, too. "That number is lower than I expected. It is sort of a letdown because I really want to work here."

Do **not say** it is less than I am making now. What you are making now or what you were making is not important to these negotiations.

If you know immediately the offer is low, your first response is to say nothing for about ten to thirty seconds. Then repeat, "$90,000 a year. I really appreciate your offer," even though you're thinking, "Ohhhh nooooo." Take the time to gather your thoughts. (This is why practicing this interviewing technique is useful.)

Here is where you can refer back to the job and say something about how much you would love working for the company. Then turn the situation into a win for both of you: "I'm sure you want to pay me a fair compensation that will keep me interested, enthusiastic and working at my peak?" (How can he disagree with that?)

You continue: "I have been doing some research and my study shows that for this kind of work with my experience and skills, the salary range is about $95,000 to $125,000." Increase the high end of your range by several thousand to give both you and Mr. Interviewer some negotiating room.

If you are entry level, increase the bottom of your range a couple of thousand. The truth is, you have less experience to offer but justifying a few extra thousand through your research may help give you some negotiation room.

Mr. Interviewer's response will be "I want to hire you, how about we reach an in-between of $105,000?" Are you willing to accept something near the middle of your range? Remember you upped it a bit. If you are, then you are happy. You just got a raise before starting work, and you got $15,000 more than you hoped for... and why?

First, because you did not talk about money until you had sold yourself. Second, you let the employer mention money first, and finally, you did your homework.

Now before we go on, would you be surprised if we said, it doesn't always work this way?

What if he doesn't say what you hoped he would?

Go back to your researched response. You could show your research to Mr. Interviewer and say: "Here is what I am basing my salary expectations on." This is where you sell your potential, enthusiasm, and willingness to work hard to Mr. Interviewer's company based on industry standards.

Mr. Interviewer is holding to his first offer.

Now the number is in your court. We agree with most experts who recommend never say no at the interview. Say, "I would really like to work here but I have to go home and think about this number, talk it over with my husband, wife, or the dog. Can I get back to you on Thursday?" (That date should never be more than two days in the future, less time is better.)

Make sure they will hold the offer until you make your decision.

Whatever you do, don't walk out of that interview without confirming the offer will be held until the time you say you will get back with them. All you need, after all your work, is to have them hire somebody else at your negotiated figure. (It happened to one of our clients. He didn't talk to us before the last interview and cooked his own goose.)

Force yourself to wait the time you asked for in the interview. Your ace in the hole is you still have the offer, lower salary number on the table. You might get more, but you know you won't get less.

Sometime before your dead line, call Mr. Interviewer with your decision. If you can, it's even better to meet with Mr. Interviewer face to face.

Sometimes you have to walk away. Sometimes, you have to take less than you want. Studies show 90 per cent of the time, reasonable, honest, and sincere negotiations bring about reasonable, honest, and sincere salary agreements.

If you decide to accept the lower offer, make sure you say you are accepting because of your desire to work for the company and your hopes for future advancement based on your abilities. "While the salary is less than I felt my qualifications are valued, I'm excited about being able to work here, and I'm confident my abilities will increase my salary in short order." Might as well let him know she has hired an ambitious and assertive employee.

Here is what is good about this whole process, even if you have to take less than you wanted because you really needed the job. You will know you tried your best to get what you wanted. You will know you have given it a great effort, and you are making a proactive decision to take the job for whatever your reasons are. It becomes an active choice rather than passive acceptance and that is always better for you, your future with this company, and especially your professional confidence.

Another piece of information about salary negotiations.

Our clients often say they think "dickering" about money could turn off an employer. We correct them, sometimes and not too gently: "Money is important both to you and the employer. If you are in the game, money is how you keep score."

We have talked to many employers about this process. One told us: "I have great respect for people who negotiate for what they want. It shows confidence, self-respect, ambition, an assertive personality, and great communication skills. These are the characteristics I thought I saw in this candidate and why I offered the job in the first place. Seeing it demonstrated in front of me, only confirms my decision."

And, no matter what the final salary is, your employer will know this about you. You have negotiated with integrity and professionalism. And, no matter what your salary, your reputation in the company starts in a respectful, professional, and positive way.

The final part to salary negotiations

Finally, the negotiation is done! What a relief. But before you walk out the door, whether you accept the offer in the office or ask to go home to think about it, get that offer in writing.

This may sound cynical. We don't mean it to be, but this is your life. You could be quitting your current job to take this one. You are basing your financial future and career on landing this job. Do not make any decision based on having the job and money you agreed on until you have a formal offer in writing. Do not quit your present job until you have your offer in writing. Do not make any financial decision based on the money you think you will be getting until you have it in writing.

Ronald Regan said: "Trust, but verify." We agree. We advise you to agree, too.

Now it's time to celebrate. On to dessert!

Teri's Famous Lemon Bars

Strawberry Pie

Inside-Out Bundt Cake

Janine's Pound Cake

Teri's Famous Lemon Bars

½-cup butter
¼-cup powdered sugar
1-cup flour
Mix ingredients like a pie crust. Pat into 9 inch by 9 inch Pyrex dish.
Bake 15 minutes at 325° or until lightly brown. Remove from oven.
Turn up oven to 350°
Topping:
3-Tablespoons lemon juice
½-teaspoon baking powder
2 eggs
1-cup sugar
3 shakes of salt
Combine ingredients pour over hot crust. Bake 25 minutes at 350°
Or until lightly browned.
Cool; then dust with a little sifted powdered sugar.

Strawberry Pie

2 TBLS corn starch
1 cup sugar
1 cup water
½ package (3oz.)
1 qt fresh strawberries
1 baked 9 inch pie shell
Whipping cream, Cool Whip
Blend together cornstarch, sugar, combine with water in saucepan. (I use the microwave). Cook until thick, about 3-5 minutes in the sauce pan
Remove from heat, add gelatin and stir until dissolved. Allow to cool, not completely cold.
Clean strawberries, slice and spread evenly in baked pie shell. Pour cooled cooked mixture over all; chill for 2-3 hours.
Garnish with whipped cream. (You can use frozen strawberries drain well.)

Inside-Out Bundt Cake

1 4 oz. package instant chocolate pudding
1 box chocolate cake mix
12 oz. chocolate chips
1 ¾ c milk
2 eggs

Combine pudding, cake mix, chips, milk and eggs in a bowl. Mix by hand until well blended about 2 minutes. Pour into a greased 10 cup Bundt pan. Bake at 350° for 50-55 minutes or until cake springs back when lightly pressed with finger. Do not over bake. Cool 15 minutes in pan. Loosen with knife. Remove from pan when totally cool.

For a special treat glaze with chocolate!
3/4 cup semisweet chocolate chips
3 tablespoons butter
1 tablespoon light corn syrup
1/4 teaspoon vanilla extract

In a double boiler over hot, but not boiling water, combine chocolate chips, butter and corn syrup. Stir until chips are melted and mixture is smooth; add vanilla.
Spread warm glaze over top of cake, letting it drizzle down the sides.

Janine's Pound Cake

Topping:
½ cup butter   1/3 cup sugar (+2 TBS.) 1 cup pecans chopped
1 ¾ cups crushed vanilla wafers

Batter:
1 cup butter   2 cups sugar   4 eggs
1 cup milk   1 ½ tsp. Vanilla   2 2/3 cups flour
1 ½ tsp. Baking powder ½ tsp. Salt

Divide topping into two loaf pans. Press down firmly and form up the side of pan. Gently add batter. Bake at 325° for 1 to 1 ½ hours, or until toothpick comes out clean.

Chapter 8

The First 90 Days...
Trying Something New

Have you ever hosted a dinner party with an international theme? That means you know that it is a great deal of work and preparation especially if you are going to try some new dishes. The party doesn't just happen. The food doesn't come together all on its own.

It's the same way with a new job. You worked hard in your job search and here you are at last: the first day on the new job. Like the international dinner party, you need to plan, plan, and plan even though you have landed. Planning is still your recipe for success.

One word of caution. Just as ovens and microwaves vary in power and intensity, each job is different. You need to be alert and calibrate yourself when you to begin your new job. Open the door to your new place of employment with the same kind of alertness and attention to detail as you bring to the first time you use a new oven. *You* will make your success happen. Be aware of your surroundings; take the time to notice everything.

Companies spend a great deal of time in the hiring process and not much time making sure the employee is on-board and successfully installed. There is often very little orientation. So be pro active (Even more after you get the job!)

Here are some tips about the first few weeks on your new job.

- When you move into a new position, now you have to hit the ground running. One useful exercise is to start planning milestones you want to make at specific times. Remember you have only ninety days to prove yourself. (Most companies have the policy, if a new hire does not work out in the first three months or ninety days, for any reason, the company can terminate without cause and it's legal.) This is why we tell you, set specific goals for yourself on your first day.

- Try to get performance expectations as early as possible, the first week is best.
- Set priorities. Ask to meet with your boss on a bi-weekly basis until you are confident you are in alignment with the job, your new responsibilities and, most importantly, the boss.
- Learn how to learn again. It might have been awhile since you have had to learn to re-learn your job. Plan to learn. Ask questions about the company history, how did people get to where they are right now? This will tell you promotion criteria. Look for people who have been around a while. They will be the best historians.
- Question everybody: customers, distributors, suppliers and, of course, associates, and your boss. Information is power. You will gain it by using the information you learn to provide yourself with actionable insights. This is information that enables you to make better decisions faster.
- Ask for an organizational chart. Find out who the go-to people are, then go to them for information.
- Learn the first names of everyone within the first week. Learn one fact about each person. (Sam rescues greyhounds, Sara has twins, and Sally bakes as a stress reliever.) Then ask them something about that fact occasionally and build on that knowledge. It will come in handy, it is relationship building, and especially important for you to blend into the company and its employees. Never stop networking.
- Learn about the whole organization, how it flows, not just how your department works. How does your department interface with people in other departments? Try to get a bigger picture.

Never, *never* say anything negative about your former bosses or your places of work. You heard that rule while you were in the job search, and it still applies. Be positive. It can only be icing on the cake now that you have the job.

- How does the staff or team communicate within the office? If it's by email and it probably is, set your computer spell check right away. Remember, email never goes away. Be careful what you put in writing and make sure you spell it right.

- Keep a log of your accomplishments. Don't expect everyone to remember all the good things you are doing when review time comes around. You might not remember them all. Keeping a log helps you see just how far you have come and helps you to update your resume.

- Be aware that you might have some new job transitioning jitters. That is very normal. You wanted this job so badly and you got it. But with it, you have to make some adjustments and you probably have some uneasy feelings. It would be unusual if you didn't. Journal those feelings and give them some attention. Take good care of yourself and keep a good life/work balance. Try not to lose yourself in your new job.

- But go slowly. Give yourself a month to get your feet on the ground in your new job. After that time, give back to those in transition. Go to a networking or professional group meeting and lend some encouragement. Stay in touch with your accountability group. Be open to change and it will change your life!

The strongest strategy in your ninety-day plan is to learn about more than just the area in which you work. It is imperative if you want to get ahead to know how the company earns its profits. Who are the important customers? Why do people do business with your company? When you know the answers to these questions, you can start to look at ways of doing your job so you are in alignment with company thinking.

Better yet, you can start being the innovative employee, the one with the big picture in mind. Innovation and big picture thinking is the epitome of human capital. Showing this style in a low-key way is good.

But go slowly. Showing it too soon sometimes sends the message; this company needs fixing or we have a new hot shot in here. Employees don't usually like to hear or see that from the new kid on the block.

If you followed our advice, you did a lot of this research when you began your job search and started looking at target companies. When you began interviewing, you did even more research; this will serve you well now. You already know a great deal about the company you learned when you were on the outside. Now confirm your information first hand from the inside.

As we say a dozen times in this book, continue to network! Network and build relationships within the company. If you got into the company through networking, nurture the relationship with the people who helped you land in this company. Working in a job is a piece of cake compared to how hard you worked to get in there. Appreciate your position.

A continuing part of your success should be staying in touch with your network. Review the networking chapter of this book. Remember how you felt when you were looking? There are still people out there who feel that way. Help them if you can.

Now let's discuss some specific tips about what kind of initial strategy you might want to adopt. Remember, this is initial. Once you get through these first ninety days, you will have your own strategy. You will have learned a lot more about how the company works and how you will work in it. However, there are some tips to get you started that are very important in the beginning. In this book, we will focus on just one issue: your boss.

As a leader, you know there are different strategies for different businesses. Managing your boss is a universal business technique and fits any business or service. Your boss can make or break you. It is that simple.

The time you invest in this critical relationship is well worth it. Your boss sets your benchmarks, interprets your actions to others, and controls access to resources and promotions. She is the gatekeeper of the promotion point. The best strategy is to negotiate some realistic expectations up front, reach a consensus, and secure enough resources and good will to succeed.

To do that requires having a ninety-day managing your boss plan. This can be done with five conversations, which you will plan and conduct with your boss. They will cover:

- The business operation
- Expectations on both sides
- Method of operation
- What you'll need for the job
- Your personal career path on the job

The first conversation is about the business operation. Once you have defined the situation, you'll need to identify your boss's role in helping you achieve results. For example, you will probably need help in getting resources, introductions, and information. This conversation will lay the groundwork for everything you do in these crucial ninety days. Ask lots of questions about how your results should look.

You might be working in a service department; all your customers are internal. How does this work? How does your boss suggest building a working relationship with another department? She may have some specific ways she interacts with the other departments. Find out the process she prefers. It is good to know preferences early.

The second conversation is about expectations — yours and your boss's. This is where you both set short-and medium-term goals and define what success is going to look like.

Together, you and your boss collaborate to decide on a timeframe for initial milestones and then look to the future beyond those targets. With this conversation, you'll be able to figure out some early wins that will align with your boss' priorities. Understanding and aligning with your boss' priorities will secure you the help you need to go to the next level. It is also smart boss management. Maybe you've heard the line, "If the boss ain't happy, ain't nobody happy." It's true.

Once you move into action, always promise slightly less than you deliver. No one will complain if you delight him with bonus results. However, promising what you cannot deliver hurts your credibility.

Frequently confirm that you are on the same page with your boss. Ask the same question in different ways to gain insight. Read between the lines. Think about how you would feel if you were the boss. You do not have to necessarily agree with your boss but you do have to understand the common goals and be working together to achieve them.

Get clear on key issues your boss is specifically interested in. Then, with your performance expectations clear, you need to understand how your boss operates so you can work together. This point is non-negotiable. You have to work well with this person. No kidding.

How does your boss operate?

For example, does your boss prefer voice mail or e-mail? Is her office door usually open or closed? Here are some behaviors to notice or ask about:

- Does she prefer talking face-to-face, exchanging emails or making phone calls?
- What kinds of decisions does she want to be involved with, and what kind will just annoy her? Ask about decision-making responsibilities, what are her preferences?
- Does she arrive early and work late?

> Take a look at your style compared to hers. What works? What doesn't? What is crucial? What will you have to change?
> Talk to others, see what they think, but do this in a very diplomatic way. Gossiping about your boss is never good.

The truth is it's your responsibility to build a good relationship with your boss and not the other way around. You are going to have to adapt to her style, whatever it is.

> If she doesn't like voice mail, don't use it. (That is pretty easy, but you have to know the preference.) We know of a case in which the employee knew what the boss wanted, yet the employee decided what the boss was doing was the wrong way to handle the situation. So he did it his own way. This is never a good way to get started in a company.
> If he wants all the details of every decision, deliver them.
> When in doubt, ask.
> If serious issues of style come up, address them directly and honestly. Clearly, this is important: The first ninety days is a trial for both you and the company. Here is the time for you to see if this is the right employment fit for you. It might not be.
> As we have said, most companies have an initiation period. This is a time when you can be fired without cause. All the company has to say is you didn't work out. And you can do the same thing. You can quit because the job wasn't what you expected. Don't be afraid to leave if it is the wrong job. You will be happier if you do it sooner rather than later.

The most important thing to remember here is you have to ask or have a conversation about how you and the boss will interact. Ask is the operative word. Conversation is collaboration. Even if you are told something you don't want to hear, the boss will know you want to do a good job. You boss will know you know the employee-boss relationship is very important, and you want to make it work. For you to be successful, your boss has to be more successful.

Once you have the boss's style figured out, think about resources. What do you need to be successful? This will vary by employer. It may not even come up. However, depending on your business it could be important. If the boss wants 10 percent growth, figure out what it will take to get it and ask for all of the resources you will need to do the job. Always link resources to clearly defined results and if you can, get it in writing.

Now, what about you and your next steps in this company?

Granted you just started here, but you are a go-getter, so your next questions are, what's most important for me to learn first? what skills do I need to develop to advance in this company? Are there special projects that could help build those skills? Ask your boss to help you define the skills you need to do an outstanding job, what skills does she think are the most important for you to develop?

We know you just started in the company and you are still in the honeymoon phase, but this conversation will open the door to more conversations and it will give your boss the idea that you want to get ahead, are eager to learn, and you can take direction. These are all good things in a new employee.

Going through each of these conversations will help you to develop a ninety-day plan. Once your boss buys into that plan, it is your ticket to success in transition. If you plan to use the first thirty days for learning and building personal credibility, make sure it's negotiated with your boss up front, and don't allow yourself to be derailed with unexpected projects.

One last tip, listen more than you talk and watch more than you do (at least at first). You are the new kid on the block; you do not know a lot of what has gone on before you got here. Ask questions. Do not try to solve problems too fast. Don't try to fit what you did in your previous company to this one yet. <u>Give yourself a chance to learn what is going on before trying to make changes.</u> Your co-workers have to get used to you just as you have to get used to them. Give both of you a chance.

Now try something new for yourself. Experiment and try an international dish. For your dining pleasure, here are some of our favorites.

Chicken-Mushroom-Spinach Quesadillas

Green Rice Pilaf

Real Lasagna

Souvlaki with Tzatziki Sauce

Chicken-Mushroom-Spinach Quesadillas

Olive oil
½ tsp. chili powder
2 garlic cloves – minced
1 tsp. oregano
½ lb. fresh spinach
8 oz. sliced mushrooms
1 ½ c shredded cooked chicken
2/3 c finely chopped onion
Sprinkle fresh cilantro
2 ½ c grated Co-Jack Cheese
Sprinkle salt & pepper (to taste)
16 small tortillas (flour)

Sauté garlic, onions and mushrooms in small amount of olive oil. Add seasonings and spinach. Sauté about 10 minutes until vegetables are browned and spinach is soft. Cool 10 minutes. Mix in chicken, cheese and season with salt & pepper. Can be made ahead of time and chilled.

Preheat grill or stovetop grill to medium heat. Lightly brush oil on 1 side of tortillas. Place tortilla oil side down on large baking sheet. Divide chicken mixture among tortillas, spreading to even thickness. Top with remaining tortillas; press together; brush lightly with oil. Grill quesadillas until heated through and golden brown about three minutes per side. Cut into wedges. Serve with a fruit salsa!

Real Lasagna

1-cup onions diced	2 Tablespoons olive oil	½-pound Italian sausage
1 pound ground round beef	1 clove garlic, minced	1-Tablespoon whole basil
1 1/2 teaspoons salt	1-1 pound can tomatoes	2 6-ounce cans tomato paste
10 ounces lasagna noodles	1 cup diced carrots	2 eggs
3 cups fresh Ricotta or cream style cottage cheese	1-cup fresh grated Parmesan cheese	
1-cup fresh Romano cheese	2 Tablespoons parsley flakes	
1-teaspoon salt	1-pound mozzarella cheese	

Sauté' onion and garlic in olive oil until onion is transparent. Add sausage and beef. Brown meat slowly. Drain off any fat.

Add basil, salt, tomatoes, tomato paste, Ricotta cheese to meat mixture. Simmer covered for about 30 minutes.

Steam carrots until soft, then add to meat mixture.

Cook noodles in large amount of boiling salted water until tender, drain, rinse in cold water.

Beat eggs. Add to meat mixture.

Layer noodles in 13x9x2 inch <u>greased</u> baking dish. Spread enough of the meat mixture to cover the lasagna noodles. Add a layer of mozzarella cheese, parmesan cheese, and Romano cheese. Repeat layering until all noodles and meat mixture is used.

Save enough mozzarella, Parmesan, and Romano to use these cheeses for the top of the lasagna.

Bake at 375° about 30 minutes or until heated through and cheese on top is melted and is a golden brown. <u>Let stand 10 minutes before cutting and serving.</u>

Assemble early and refrigerate, bake about 45 minutes.

This dish can also be made ahead and frozen. Thaw in refrigerator one day before baking.

Makes about 10 servings.

Souvlaki with Tzatziki Sauce

3 tablespoons fresh lemon juice
1/2 teaspoon dried oregano
2 tablespoons olive oil
Salt and Pepper to taste
4 garlic cloves, mashed
1 white onion sliced
1/2 pound tender boneless pork, cut into 1-inch pieces
Prepare Souvlaki by combining first 5 ingredients in a zip-top plastic bag; seal and shake to combine. Add pork and onions; seal and shake to coat. Allow to marinate in refrigerator for 30 minutes, turning once. Remove pork and onions from bag; discard marinade. Coat a 12" skillet with olive oil and cook pork and onions over medium heat until meat is done, turning once. Do not overcook.

Tzatziki Sauce
1/2 cup cucumber, peeled, seeded, and shredded
1/2 cup plain low-fat yogurt
1 tablespoon lemon juice
1/4 teaspoon salt
1 garlic clove, minced
To prepare tzatziki sauce, combine cucumber, yogurt, lemon juice, salt, and garlic clove, stirring well. Serve the Tzatziki sauce with Souvlaki and Pita Bread.

Now get going............

We have given you some ideas about finding a job and then making a smooth transition to your new job. You know the one you worked so hard to find. Finding a job is a job. It is one of the hardest jobs you will ever have. As we have said many times in the book - *we understand*. We hope we softened the stress of the search a little by giving you good solid job search ideas sprinkled with homely humor and good food ideas.

Our experience tells us if you know what you are doing, have a full stomach and a big smile, life just goes a lot easier.

As you move forward in your career, we gave you the tools for a more productive job search with some good recipes to enjoy while you are searching. Of course, that doesn't mean it will be a piece of cake (even our cake) because it won't be. We want you to take care of yourself while you are going through the search process because taking care of yourself WILL make the search easier, we promise.

We hope we gave you a smile or two and when you take a break (and we hope you do) try some of our recipes. We promise the search will be easier if you do. Take some time to take care of yourself. Eat, laugh, have some fun, meet people and build relationships. Find your dream job and live your life fully. We believe in making a life as well as making a living.

Do all the things we suggest to secure your next job. Refer to us often... We would like to think we are right beside you in your search. Now get going; land your next job and along the way cook and smile while you develop *"A Taste for Work."*